An Electrifying History
Public Service Co. of New Hampshire

Arthur M. Kenison

An Electrifying History

Designed & Published by
Oak Manor Publishing, Inc..
Manchester, NH 03102

Printed and bound in the United State of America by
Minuteman Press of Nashua
88 Main Street
Nashua, NH 03060
603-883-4890
Fax: 603-883-4893

May 2004
ISBN 0-9747361-0-4

Library of Congress Data applied for.

COVER PHOTO Courtesy of The Nashua Historical Society. All other photos courtesy of PSNH or the author unless otherwise noted with the photo.

Kenison, Arthur M.
Electrifying New Hampshire: Public Service Co. of New Hampshire/Arthur M. Kenison
p. cm.
Includes bibliographic references and index
ISBN 0-9747361-0-4
1.Public Service Co. of New Hampshire 2. Electric Utilities 3. Business History-New Hampshire 4. Business History-United States.

CIP

Raven, this one's for you.

Acknowledgments

Many institutions and individuals were helpful in assisting me with the writing of this book. First, I wish to thank Public Service Co. of New Hampshire for granting me limited access to its archives. I am particularly grateful for the company's willingness to provide factual data without attempting to direct the conclusions reached in this work.

Second, I wish to acknowledge Saint Anselm College for providing me with a summer research grant to work on this project. Third, my thanks to the libraries at the Manchester Historic Association, the New Hampshire Historical Society, the City of Manchester and the State of New Hampshire.

The individuals that I wish to thank and cite their contributions are numerous. A special thanks to O.R. Cummings, the trolley historian, for all of his attempts to educate me on railway history and operations. Next I wish to thank many individuals associated with Public Service Co. of New Hampshire: Martin Murray, for assisting me in understanding the world of deregulation; Barbara Doyle, for her guidance in researching PSNH's archives; Owen McQueeney, a former PSNH employee, for his useful insight; and Bill Frain and Gary Long, prior and current PSNH presidents, for granting me interviews.

I am indebted to many colleagues at Saint Anselm College: John Romps, for his analysis on the Seabrook bankruptcy; David Guerra, for assisting me in explaining the various technical aspects of water and electric power; Thomas Lee, for his input on the ecological impact of the Seabrook Nuclear Plant; Austin Conley, for his meticulous review of my writing; Robert Perreault, for his careful review as to the historical accuracy of my writing; Fay Tresvik and my wife Jeanne Kenison for their helpful critiques of my work; and Barbara Miller for her assistance in gathering the various illustrations in the book.

Just as old men boast about their children and grandchildren, old professors bask in the glory of former students. It is with great pride I thank Todd Bohan, a graduate of Saint Anselm College, who went on to earn a Ph.D. and currently is working in the utility industry, for his insights and guidance on regulation.

Finally, I particularly wish to thank John Greene who somehow manages to turn my meager efforts into a finished product.

Arthur M. Kenison
Hampton, New Hampshire
May 2004

Table of Contents

Manchester's first street car.

Chapter 1

Biography of a Corporation

When one reaches a milestone of seventy-five or one hundred years, whether it is an individual or a business institution, it is a time to reflect on past accomplishments and failures. Public Service Co. of New Hampshire and its predecessor Manchester Traction, Light and Power Co. are no exception. The original organization was incorporated in August 1901. Twenty-five years later, in August 1926, the firm was reorganized as Public Service Co. of New Hampshire. In a broader sense, this is the history of electricity in New Hampshire inasmuch as PSNH is synonymous with electricity within the state.

This work can be viewed as representative of the growth of electric utilities across the nation. Much of the history is typical of that repeated throughout the United States. Often electric service began with several firms competing in a single community. Like Manchester Traction, these competing firms were often united by investment bankers hoping to reap the rewards of the elimination of wasteful duplication of equipment and the lowering of costs associated with economies of scale. When the quest for further benefits from scale size led to expansion beyond a local community, this was often done by national public utility holding companies. Public Service Co. of New Hampshire, like other operating utilities throughout the country, wrestled free from the holding company grasp after the 1929 stock market crash.

Like its sister utilities throughout the country, Public Service Co.

of New Hampshire emerged from the Great Depression stronger than industrial companies. Electric companies across the United States continued to merge in the quest to provide better and lower cost service. Such was the case for PSNH, servicing 70 percent of the state by 1950. At this point, like other electric firms, Public Service Co. of New Hampshire fought the battle against the movement for government ownership of its industry. In the second half of the twentieth century, electric utilities played a major part in the growth of their local economy. PSNH was no exception. The search for alternative energy sources was repeated throughout the country. What was atypical was the cost paid by Public Service Co. of New Hampshire's constituents, its customers, its workers and its stockholders, as a result of building the Seabrook nuclear plant.

This current book attempts to provide the reader with a chronology of the history of Manchester Traction, Light and Power Co. and its successor Public Service Co. of New Hampshire. The goal is to make the reader question why a given decision was made. Hopefully it is written in an objective manner differentiating facts from opinions. When opinions are presented, diverse views are given, allowing the readers to draw their own conclusions on various controversial events. The primary purpose of historical inquiry should be the assessment of the events studied. With this in mind an epilogue at the end of the book will suggest how certain historical events covered in the book may be of assistance in understanding contemporary events in business in general and regulated industries in particular.

On the other hand, history should be fun. For that reason, many anecdotal incidents will be included. In addition, the book will highlight some of the companies' management and employees that were responsible for the past performance. Ultimately, the conscience of a corporation can be no better or no worse than the consciences of the men and women who direct its behavior.

Good biographies of individuals frequently begin with a chapter surveying the ancestral lineage of the person being studied. They often trace two and three generations highlighting those predecessors and events that shaped the individual under study. The same can be said for corporate histories. The men who organized and ran these early firms had as great an impact on the managers of Manchester Traction,

Light and Power Co. as parents and grandparents would have on an individual. In a similar manner the founding managers of Manchester Traction had their impact on the subsequent generations that would assume their roles for Public Service Co. of New Hampshire. This is particularly true in firms that believed in promotion from within.

The reader unfamiliar with early methods of mass transportation may question what a horse-powered railway system has to do with a modern utility company. The high school reader may be as dumbfounded as this author was when he would enter the electric utility's retail store to purchase his school bus tokens some 45 years ago. Other activities under the utility's umbrella included running a summer theater that hosted vaudeville acts, and an amusement park with roller skating, a penny arcade and roller coaster.

What do horses, buses, vaudeville and penny arcades have in common with an electric company? The answer lies in the method of public transportation that fell between the horse-drawn railway and the diesel-powered buses and the reason why the summer theater and amusement park were built. But this is subject matter for the next chapter.

Early street car on Elm Street. (Courtesy Manchester Historic Association)

Chapter 2

Predecessor Corporations

In the last quarter of the nineteenth century Manchester, New Hampshire, had no intracity public transportation. While residents could travel between cities by steam railroads such as the Manchester and Lawrence Railroad and the Concord Railroad, there was no convenient public method of travel within the city. That all changed on Saturday, September 15, 1877, when over the course of the day, 700 people paid five cents each to take a horse-drawn railroad ride down Elm Street. The line which began at the corner of Webster and Elm Streets traveled south on Elm to Granite Street where it turned west crossing the Merrimack River. The line then turned south on to South Main Street. The tracks covered a distance of 2.4 miles. The following day the number swelled to more than 1,300 people. Thus began operations of the Manchester Horse Railroad. The company had been incorporated in 1871 some six years earlier, but it was not until June of 1877 that construction began in earnest.

The concept of a horse-drawn street railway was not original to Manchester. In fact, the first such system dates back to December 22, 1831, when the City of New York granted a charter to the New York and Harlem Railroad Co. The line, which began operation in the fall of 1832, traveled along New York's Fourth Avenue from Twenty-third Street to the Harlem River. As might be expected, other major cities followed New York's lead.

The installation of Manchester Horse Railroad's rails served two useful purposes. The first and obvious purpose was the reduction of friction which allowed a single horse to pull a much larger load. The second less obvious purpose was the establishment of a defined route. Once the public became aware of the time schedule, they became accustomed to leaving their homes, walking three or four blocks to the closest stop on the route, and then hopping the railway to their downtown destination.

Three of the original directors and officers of the Manchester Horse Railroad, Ezekiel A. Straw, Frederick Smyth and James A. Weston had previously served as governors of New Hampshire. Their interest in the project seemed to be motivated primarily by a desire to provide the public with a means of transportation rather than for personal financial gain.

Straw, the railroad's first president, began his career as an assistant civil engineer with the Nashua-Lowell Railway. In 1838 he was hired by the Amoskeag Manufacturing Company to assist in the construction of the canals and turbine wheels for the corporation's water power system. In the years prior to the development of electricity, textile firms used belt-driven machinery. Amoskeag, like most other New England textile mills, built their factories on the river bank just below a fall in the river. A dam would be constructed to divert a portion of river flow to a canal or series of canals. The mills would be located between the canal and the river. Portions of the canal water would be diverted through various channels, located under the mills, back to the river. In these channels, turbines would be attached to vertical shafts that would rise the entire height of the mill. The water rushing through the turbines, past the fins caused the vertical shafts to rotate. At each floor a set of gears attached to the vertical shafts would set in motion the rotation of horizontal shafts that ran the length of the building. The rotation of the horizontal shafts would then activate the various textile machines through a series of leather belts that ran from the shafts to the machines. The potential of harnessing the power of New England rivers was the reason for the rapid growth of textile firms in that section of the country.

In 1858, Ezekiel Straw was chosen as the agent, or chief operations officer of Amoskeag. During his tenure in that position, he assisted in laying the foundation which allowed Amoskeag to become the world's largest cotton textile business. Straw was the first of three generations of his family to hold this position. While Mr. Straw's

Ezekiel Straw   *Charles Williams*

primary employment was with Amoskeag, he was continuously active in the development and improvement of Manchester. He represented that city in both branches of the legislature prior to being elected to a two-year term as governor of the state in 1872. Straw served in these government positions concurrently with his association with Amoskeag.

Straw's role as president of the Manchester Horse Railroad, toward the end of his career, appears to have been motivated for public good. In those days, the title of president usually was designated to what one now might refer to as the chair of the board of directors. Frequently this position did not involve any direct association with the day to day management. The chief executive officer of New England corporations usually held the title of treasurer with the chief operating officer taking the title of either general manager or agent. It is interesting to note that Straw had served as one of the original directors of the Manchester Gas Co., when it was organized in 1851, some twenty-six years earlier.

Because of ill health, Straw resigned as agent of Amoskeag in 1878. Over the next two years he resigned from his board positions with Amoskeag and the Manchester Horse Railroad. Tributes to his contribution to Amoskeag toward the end of his career by William Amory, the company's treasurer, highlight Straw's talents:

> ...Preeminently fitted by nature and education to excel in the management of the affairs of a company... by his exceptional facility of orga-

nization... his keen insight into human nature and instinctive power over men, and then by his marvelous luck, that element in his character so difficult to define, and so essential to success, and such a subtle compound of merit, good fortune and faith, so nicely and cunningly blended that you can neither analyze nor dissolve it.

If a mill foundation was to be laid in April, and the mill itself to be hurried into completion before the close of the season for outdoor work, an early spring and a late winter were to be vouchsafed to his wishes and prophesy. If a leak or other injury to a canal made a Sunday's job a work of necessity, even though a desecration of the Sabbath, he was providentially favored by a fine day and moonlight night. If a dam across the river at the falls or a river wall along the channel of the stream had to be built, a long summer's drought was graciously granted to his predictions and hopes, and when, by a miracle and a wall, the water turned on one side into the land, and in order to restore the width of the river it was necessary on the opposite side, by another miracle to turn the land into the water, he had only to stake out the ground and invoke the destructive power of an April freshet, and the floods came and the rains descended, and it was done by the twinkling of an eye, without cost to the Company and with such mathematical precision as to almost create a superstitious impression of his possessing some mysterious control over the elements.

Despite the limited time that Straw was associated with the horse railroad, his prestige and strength of character made a lasting contribution to its development.

The original horse railway cars had seating capacity for sixteen passengers, and ran every fifteen minutes from 6:00 A.M. to 9:00 P.M., Monday through Saturday. The Sunday schedule began at 9:00 A.M. The service was immediately welcomed by the city's residents, who expressed desire for both an extension of the original line and the establishment of new lines. Construction on subsequent railroad lines and the purchase of additional cars rapidly followed. By 1887, ten years after the original line was laid, nine miles of tracks throughout the primary byways of the city provided the public with access to this new method of public transportation. To insure the possibility of operating throughout the year, the company purchased a large snow plow constructed explicitly for its use by the Manchester Locomotive Works.

In 1889, Charles Williams gained control of the Manchester Horse

Railroad when he purchased the shares owned by Frederick Smyth and James Weston, two of the original directors, and the estate of Samuel N. Bell. Bell, who had served as president of the railroad since 1880, had recently passed away. Williams, who was a director of the Nashua Street Railway took over the management of the firm which he renamed the Manchester Street Railway. While the prior owners had been investigating the possibility of electrifying the system just prior to Bell's untimely death, Williams felt that the current electric technology was too uncertain to justify such an investment at that time. The first electrified rail line was constructed in Germany in 1881. However, it was not until 1888 that Frank J. Sprague organized the first successful United States public trolley system in Richmond, Virginia.

In 1895, six years after Williams purchased the horse railroad, the Manchester Street Railway was electrified. When a horse-drawn railway was electrified, the procedure was to either build a power plant or to purchase electricity from a local producer. Electricity would be transmitted along a wire suspended above the tracks of the railway. The cars were equipped with a trolley, or bar with a wheel on the end, which would make contact with the electrified wire. A spring system would apply pressure to the bar to ensure that the trolley wheel would ride along the electrified wire from below. The energy would run two motors located below the cars causing the wheels to rotate. The motorman could vary the current flow to the motors to change speeds. The electric circuit would be completed by the rails which provided the ground return to the power source. The Manchester project required an investment financed by the sale of $250,000 worth of mortgage bonds. On June 8 the first electric trolley traveled from Traction Street to the North End. By the end of the year all of the company's existing lines were electrified. That same year, the company sold $190,000 of new stock to finance the construction of additional trackage and to reduce company debt. Despite the improvement in service, the fare remained at five cents. In fact it remained at that level until the inflation associated with World War I forced the firm to raise the rate to six and then eight cents.

The street railway contracted with the Manchester Electric Light Co. to provide the necessary power. The Manchester Electric Light

Co. was incorporated in 1881 for the express purpose of providing outdoor arc lighting to the city. However, the firm was unsuccessful in selling a sufficient number of shares to generate the required funds to cover the cost of construction. The following year, the New England Weston Electric Light Co. of Boston stepped in to provide the city with the proposed street lighting. The Boston firm subcontracted the original power from the Amoskeag Manufacturing Company's electric facilities while it began construction of its own steam power electric plant in Manchester. Originally, all of Amoskeag's belt-driven looms were powered by water turbines from its canal system. However, in the 1880s when its power requirements had outgrown the capacity of the river, Amoskeag began to utilize both steam-driven belt systems and steam-generated electricity.

On April 23, 1882, New England Weston Electric Light Co. turned on the first electric arc street lights in Manchester. This occurred some two weeks prior to the completion of Thomas Edison's famous Pearl Street Station in New York City that amazed the world by illuminating streets and buildings in a portion of lower Manhattan. The following year, New England Weston Electric Light Co. completed the construction of its Manchester steam power plant and began generating power from its Brook Street location. Coal was used to heat the water in the boiler until it produced high-pressure steam. The expanding steam was directed through the turbine causing the fins to rotate. The turbine was attached to an armature composed of coils of wire. The rotation of the armature within a magnetic field generated the electricity. Two years later in 1885, New England Weston Electric Light Co. transferred the Brook Street plant to the Manchester Electric Co.

By 1895, the year Manchester Street Railway had contracted with Manchester Electric Light Co. to supply the necessary power, there were no less than five additional electric companies organized to provide energy to the greater-Manchester area. The first of these was the Ben Franklin Electric Co. which was incorporated in 1886. This facility provided steam-generated electricity from its location at the Manchester Gas Co. It is uncertain as to whether this subsidiary was organized by the gas company to insure its survival, if the future illumination would be dominated by electricity. What is known is that the new corporation had the same board of directors and management.

The second firm, the Electric Co., was organized in 1890 and generated hydroelectric power from its Kelley's Falls location. Hydroelectric power can be pictured as a cross between the belt-driven energy found at Amoskeag and the steam-driven electric energy being produced by Manchester Electric Co. at its Brook Street Station. A

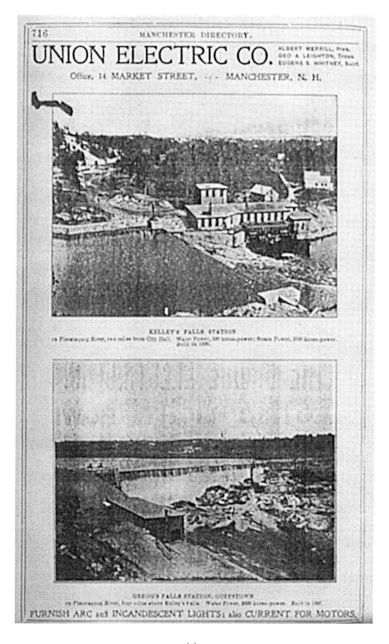

716   MANCHESTER DIRECTORY.

UNION ELECTRIC CO.

ALBERT MERRILL, Pres.
GEO A LEIGHTON, Treas.
EUGENE E. WHITNEY, Supt.

Office, 14 MARKET STREET, - - MANCHESTER, N. H.

KELLEY'S FALLS STATION

FURNISH ARC and INCANDESCENT LIGHTS; also CURRENT FOR MOTORS.

hydroelectric plant would be located near the fall in a river. A dam would be constructed and a portion of the water would be diverted through channels where turbines were located. The turbines would cause the attached shaft to rotate. However, rather than directly activating machinery from a belt system, the revolution would be used to cause an attached conducting loop of wires to rotate within a magnetic field generating the desired electricity.

A third firm, the Merrimack Electric Light, Heat and Power Co. was incorporated in 1891. That firm began selling electricity from its Hooksett location in 1895. The fourth firm, the Garvin's Falls Power Co. began producing hydroelectric power in 1892. The final firm, the Union Electric Co. was organized in 1893 at which time it absorbed the Electric Co. In effect, the industry was characterized as competitive with easy entry into a market with no apparent economies of scale.

This multiplicity of firms was not particular to Manchester. Similar situations were found throughout the country. The redundancy of firms did not completely characterize the competitiveness of the industry. In addition to competition among electric power firms selling electricity, they faced the additional competition from firms such as Amoskeag that produced its own power from either hydroelectric or coal-driven steam-powered electricity. In fact, there was a difference of opinions between the leading innovators and manufacturers of electrical generating machinery as to the ultimate future of electric energy. One school of thought headed by the Thomson-Houston firm believed the future was in selling its machinery to manufacturing firms to generate its own electricity. The second school led by the Edison General Electric Co. espoused that the central station providing electricity to the community would be the most economical and practical method.

Competition among Manchester's electric firms was reduced significantly in 1892 when the Manchester Electric Light Co. purchased the Ben Franklin Electric Co. Perhaps the most valuable asset that Manchester Electric Light Co. acquired was the services of J. Brodie Smith. Smith originally moved to Manchester from New York State in 1880 to work as a pharmacist in his brother's drug store. As a youth in New York, Smith found an interest in electricity. He began

First passengers to Lake Massabesic pose to honor the occasion.

studying the subject and conducting his own experiments. It was not long before his avocation became his vocation. He soon left the pharmacy to do electrical contracting. In 1886 when the Ben Franklin Electric Co. was organized, J. Brodie Smith was its manager. In 1893, the year following the acquisition of the Ben Franklin Electric Co. by the Manchester Electric Light Co., J Brodie Smith was appointed superintendent of the consolidated firms.

In 1895, the same year that the Manchester Street Railway electrified its existing lines, it opened one new line. This traveled from downtown Manchester to Massabesic Lake. This line was a seasonal operation. While the other lines of the company were directed to the utilitarian purpose of providing a means of transportation for work and shopping, travel on the new route was primarily for pleasure. The fare for the lake run was ten cents, or double the rate for all other lines. To enhance the enjoyment of a day at the lake, the firm constructed a pavilion later the same year. This branch met with immediate profitability with cars often running with standing room only. Four years later, Manchester Street Railway built a summer theater, which hosted vaudeville acts and musical comedies.

Ultimately, this line would serve as a boom to land developers and citizens of the city in search of housing. The line extended the reasonable commuting distance from the central city, encouraging eastward expansion.

In 1896, the Manchester Electric Co. was formed. Over the next four years, this firm would absorb Garvin's Falls Power Co., Union Electric Co., Merrimack Electric Light, Heat and Power Co., and Consolidated Electric Co., an additional power company incorporated in 1899. The amalgamation of these firms ultimately reduced the number of independent power companies to two: Manchester Electric Light Co. and Manchester Electric Co.

In his 1976 work on the history of Public Service Co. of New Hampshire, Everett B. Sackett states two innovations by these predecessors in the last decade of the nineteenth century that were critical to the long-run success of Public Service:

> In December 1890, the company [Manchester Electric Light] put into operation the first alternating current generator... The year 1891 saw another innovation, the first electric motor for power purposes. This was installed to run the press of the Saturday Telegram at its plant on Hanover Street... These two developments, the industrial use of electric power and alternating current, opened the way for the future development of PSNH. Fifty years later, power for industrial use accounted for more than half of the sales of the Company. The ready transforming of alternating current from high voltage for long distance transmission to low voltage for local distribution made feasible two things: the construction of generating plants at sites where water power was available even though removed from centers of population; and the interconnecting of power lines over a wide area.

On December 31, 1899, as Manchester celebrated the birth of a new century under the lights of Elm Street, its population had much reason for optimism. The mills, which provided the community with a major portion of its employment, had an international reputation for the quality of its output. The community had a reliable, electrified city rail system that not only provided transportation to and from work, but also had a line to take its residents for a day at the lake. Each year more households were replacing their gas lights with electricity provided by one of the city's two electric companies. Some were experimenting with electricity to power machines or to provide heat. Soon this new power source would be applied to assisting various functions around the home. Sewing machines would be electrified. Electric irons or ironers, as they were then called, would make the chores associated with Monday's washing easier. Electric fans would cool the house.

Manchester's arches of light, 1912

Chapter 3

A Single Power Company

In 1898, Tucker, Anthony & Co., a Boston-based investment firm, acquired control of the Manchester Street Railway through the purchase of its 17,000 shares, of which all but forty-one were owned by Charles Williams. Tucker, Anthony & Co. paid $175 per share, or just less than $3 million. The following year the investment firm also gained control of Manchester's two remaining electric companies under its New England Electric Power Co. J. Brodie Smith was appointed the superintendent of the Manchester Street Railways, indicating Tucker, Anthony & Co.'s plan to run the combined electrical producers and the city's primary consumer as one entity.

In 1901, Manchester Traction, Light and Power Co., under the direction of the Boston investing firm, absorbed the various electric producers into one corporation. The Manchester Street Railway was controlled by 100 percent stock ownership. However, for all practical matters, the organizations ran as a single unit. As might be expected, the Boston Investors W.A. Tucker and S. Reed Anthony assumed the positions of president and treasurer. J. Brodie Smith, the former pharmacist, was in charge of all local operations with the title of general manager. Similar amalgamations were being repeated throughout the United States as the industry began to realize the potential for reducing costs with the construction of larger power plants.

The following year, Manchester Traction, Light and Power opened Pine Island Park at the end of the Goffs Falls branch of the Street Railway. The company purchased an estate there. A lake was formed by damming the Cohas Brook that ran through the property. The advertisement of the company in the city directory highlighted this project as follows:

This beautiful pleasure resort, maintained in connection with the street railway, is one of the most popular amusement centers in the state and inland bathing resorts. It contains a large roller skating rink, dance hall, boat landing, with fleet of canoes, roller coaster, penny arcade, merry-go-round, a whip, a dodgem, and many other popular forms of amusement. One of the large islands may be reserved for pleasure parties on request, free of charge.

For today's reader, who has experienced Disney World, Six Flags or Busch Gardens, this may appear meager. However, for a mill worker in 1902, with a sixty-hour work week and little discretionary income, this offered unheard of recreation. It was not unusual for traction companies in the larger cities throughout the country to develop similar projects. In addition to the revenue generated from the amusements, many of which were heavy users of electric power, it increased traffic on the trolleys particularly on weekends when traditionally the volume was weakest.

For the same reason, MTL&P continued to encourage ridership on its Massabesic Lake Line by hosting vaudeville acts at its summer theater. The procedure was to contract with theatrical agents, such as J.W. Gorman and R.L. Gorman of Boston. The arrangements called for a sharing of the ticket revenue after a minimum was reached. As might be expected, the contracts were explicit on the type of shows the traction company felt appropriate. Typical wording included:

[T]o furnish amusement attractions at Massabesic Lake Summer Theater... during the summer season of 1909, two shows daily, matinee and evening, for a period of twelve weeks, . . . the entertainment to be of a refined and moral character and satisfactory to said Railway, all to be presented in a high class way.

18

A trolley arrives at Pine Island Park. *(Courtesy of O.R. Cummings)*

In addition to overseeing the operations of Pine Island Park and the Massabesic Lake Summer Theater, J. Brodie Smith led Manchester Traction, Light and Power into intercity transportation when it opened up separate lines to Nashua and Derry which were operated as two new subsidiary corporations. The first new corporation, the Manchester and Nashua Street Railway began operations on January 1, 1907. To go from downtown Manchester to downtown Nashua cost twenty-five cents. There was a five-cent local fare from the city hall to the end of the Goffs Falls line. The rider then passed through three five-cent zones before reaching the Nashua Street railway where a final five-cent fare was required to reach Tremont Square in Nashua. The eighteen-mile trip had a fifty-five minute running time. Once this line was established, it was theoretically possible to travel all the way from New York City to Concord, New Hampshire by trolleys. However

Pine Island Park, about 1910.

because of the time involved, as opposed to the more rapid travel by steam railroads, this was not a practical alternative for such an extended trip.

Construction on the Manchester and Derry Street Railroad began on April 8, just three months after the opening up of the Manchester and Nashua line. On November 30, the new company began service. The fare from downtown Manchester to West Derry was fifteen cents, consisting of a

Situations as this, which demonstrated the demand for electricity in downtown Manchester, forced MTL&P to move wiring underground.

local fare of five cents to the end of the Goffs Falls line, five cents to North Londonderry and a final five cents to West Derry. This thirteen-mile trip had a forty-five-minute running time. Because of the limited population along this line, the railway never generated sufficient profits. To economize, the schedule was reduced to being hourly instead of every fifteen-minutes.

In 1907, independent of Manchester Traction, a group of local businessmen formed a company to build and operate a cable car line on Mount Uncanoonuc in Goffstown, New Hampshire. In the evolution of streetcars across the nation, the cable car emerged between the horse-drawn railroad and the trolley cars. Appropriately, the first city to claim the operation of a steam-powered cable system was San Francisco. In 1873, Andrew S. Hallidie, a wire rope manufacturer, devised a system in which a continuous cable was be activated through a conduit below the street. The cable car was equipped with a gripping clamp which extended through a slot in the pavement. The operator, called a gripman, would activate and deactivate the connection with the moving cable to run or stop the car. This new method was adopted by many of the major cities in the United States. By 1907, most of the cable systems across the country had been replaced by trolleys.

Because of the need for a rapid elevation up the mountain, a cable car line was chosen as opposed to a streetcar system. However, unlike the early city cable systems, the Uncanoonuc cable system was powered by electricity. It had a second major difference from the conventional city system. In the typical urban system, the cable would be constantly running. The motorman would stop the trolley by disengaging the car from the cable. The motorman would allow passengers to enter and exit the trolley, then reconnect the trolley to the moving cable. Because of the particular nature of the limited run in the Uncanoonuc system, two cable cars were permanently attached to the cable in such a manner that when one was at the top the other was at the cable station at the foot of the mountain. When the cable system was activated, the cars would meet each other at the halfway point of the route, where the tracks doubled allowing them to pass. With the advent of the new transportation system, the mountain became a location for summer homes. One of the residents was J. Brodie Smith. While the Uncanoonuc purchased its power from Manchester Traction, Power and Light Co., it never became a part of the Manchester Street Railway system.

Manchester Traction had been profitable from its inception. It had little difficulty meeting its 6 percent dividend requirements on its $2.8 million of stock. In 1906 the rate was increased to 7 percent. The following year it was permanently increased to 8 percent, with a 5 percent extra dividend paid in 1912.

By 1909 the revenue from the power and light portion of the

business exceeded trolley income. At the same time, the firm was expanding the geographical area that it provided light and power.

In 1911 the State of New Hampshire passed legislation creating a Public Service Commission. Prior to this date the only industries under state regulation were railroads and traction firms. This appears to be the reason that Manchester Traction, Light and Power controlled its trolley systems through subsidiary corporations. In addition to absorbing the duties of the previous Railroad Commission, this new body was responsible for regulating electric, gas, water and telephone companies. The commission's responsibilities included authorization of plant expansions, approving new stock and bond issues and setting of new rates. It is interesting to note that one of the first non-railroad matters that the commission acted on was the request of Keene Gas and Electric Co., one of the firms united with Manchester Traction when Public Service Co. of New Hampshire was formed in 1926. The Keene firm requested permission to form a subsidiary corporation, Ashuelot Gas and Electric Co. The new firm was created to establish transmission lines from the Connecticut River to Keene.

The following year the commission published the first summary of statistics for electric firms throughout the state. There was a total of sixty-seven firms. Manchester Traction was by far the largest, with 22 percent of the statewide sales and 34 percent of the industry's profit. This more than proportional share of profit was a result of the economies associated with larger output.

In his 1950 Newcomen address, "Amber Forever," Avery R. Schiller, then president of PSNH made the following observations on the subjects of consolidations and regulation:

> By the end of the nineteenth century competing electric companies had been built up in many different localities, including Manchester... Fortunately, it was soon recognized that serving the public with Electricity is not the type of enterprise which can be carried on successfully from any point of view with rival companies competing with each other. The duplication of investment and facilities imposed costs and problems which more than offset any possible advantage. It, therefore, was inevitable and proper that there should come a time when competing electric companies should consolidate with a corresponding growth in strength, size, and future potential of the survivors. Of course this resulted in the creation of

monopolies, so it equally was inevitable and proper that there should be some restraining influence and control over these monopolies. As a result there has developed wisely over the years, regulation by commissions and other agencies of the type, we have today.

It is interesting to look back on the pre-consolidation days and to note how few of the early companies made much money... At the same time, it is only fair to add that many of those then connected with the industry seemed more interested in the possibilities of a capital gain resulting from a sale [of stock] than in income [from providing electricity].

In 1913, total revenue, which included both electricity and traction sales, exceeded $1 million for the first time. Two years later, the company made an offer to stockholders of Nashua Light, Heat & Power Co. to exchange one share of the Nashua company for one share of Manchester Traction, Light & Power Co. and $40 in cash. Nashua's revenue was approximately 22 percent of the Manchester firm's sales. In an address given in 1951, Avery Schiller made the following comments on the origin of this company:

Known as the Nashua Electric Light Co., it was incorporated by seven citizens of the Gate City who subscribed $1,000 each and borrowed the necessary additional funds to establish an operating plant. They built a three-story building on Water Street, using the bottom floor for the engine, dynamo, and boilers. The upper floors were occupied by a paper box shop... The plant began operations in December 1886, facing a terrific problem to find customers for its output. In those days street lighting was the primary outlet for electricity but the gas company effectively blocked any contract with the City for such lighting. Success began to come, however, when James H. Tolles, one of the incorporators, was elected mayor of the city. In his regime, a contract for the street lighting was made and things began to improve from then on but it was a long hard trial to success.

The firm went on to acquire the Nashua Gas Light Co. at which time it changed its name. By the time of the merger, Nashua Light, Heat and Power Co. provided all the electric and gas business in Nashua and Hudson, New Hampshire. In 1917 that firm was absorbed into Manchester Traction. In the process, Manchester Traction entered the gas business in the Nashua area.

In April 1915, Manchester Traction experienced competition from jitney services. One firm headed by Mrs. E.A. Rogers provided 5-

Manchester Traction Streetcar.

cent automobile rides along Elm Street between Webster and Granite Streets. Since the price was equal to that charged by Manchester Traction, the decision as to which system to take was based on whether a trolley or jitney arrived first. Since the jitney ride was limited to Elm Street, it was not in competition for rides off the main street.

However, an alternative jitney service started about the same time proved to be a more serious competitor. The trolley system provided service to the northwest section of the city from the downtown center by first heading south, turning west to cross the Granite Street Bridge, at which point it would then head north and west. Jitney operators soon discovered that they could cut several minutes off the commuting time by providing direct service from the city center by crossing the MacGregor Bridge at the north end of the city center. While the jitney's price, five cents, was the same as Manchester Traction, it had the advantage providing quicker service. This jitney program to the northwest section of the city ultimately resulted in a buses run under the corporate name of Notre Dame Bus Line, Inc.

In 1915, Manchester Traction increased its capital stock to $3.7

million from its previous $2.8 million. The proceeds generated from this new stock issue were used to finance the purchase of the stock of the Nashua company. Two years later in 1917, Manchester Traction formerly absorbed Nashua Light, Heat and Power Co., severing its independent corporate status. That same year, the capital stock was further increased to $3.9 million through a rights offering to existing shareholders. Under a rights offering, the new stock is offered at a discount below the current market price to existing stockholders on a prorated basis. The rationale was to insure that those stockholders who wished to exercise their rights and purchase additional shares, would maintain their proportional ownership in the firm. Those stockholders electing not to purchase the additional shares could sell the rights to individuals wishing to purchase the new shares.

The proceeds generated from the new stock issue were intended to finance additional expansions. In 1919, company revenue exceeded $2 million. It was only six years earlier that sales passed the $1 million level. In 1920 the capital stock was further increased to $4.2 million as the company expanded its service to additional communities in the Manchester and Nashua area. In addition to new stock issues, the firm acquired equity capital through an increase in retained earnings, i.e., that portion of net income not distributed as dividends. Over the five-year period ending in fiscal year 1920, that number grew by $500,000 to $1.4 million.

Power facilities in 1923 consisted of four waterpower developments with a combined capacity of 9,400 kilowatts. Steam power plants provided Manchester Traction with additional capacity of 14,000 kilowatts. Service to the surrounding communities was provided by 66 miles of transmission lines and 1,540 miles of distribution lines. The daily gas capacity at the Nashua plant was 900,000 cubic feet.

By 1925, the year prior to the amalgamation into Public Service Co. of New Hampshire, Manchester Traction, Light and Power Co.'s revenue, which included service to Nashua and 17 other communities in the Manchester-Nashua area, had grown to $2.6 million. To support this operation, electric capacity was increased to 33,450 kilowatts. The company had 22,314 electric meters and 6,449 gas meters for a total customer base of 28,763. This was a growth of 12 percent from the prior year. However, the 9.2 million passengers carried on its transit system was down 13 percent from the previous year. While the power business was growing, transportation was declining as more and more people were purchasing automobiles.

The continual expansion over the twenty-five years was financed by periodic additional stock sales to the point that the total shares outstanding was just under its $5 million authorized capital. Throughout its life as a separate corporation, the company maintained an appropriate balance of debt. Both its stock and bonds always were ranked as investment grade, and the firm never missed a dividend on its common stock.

Throughout its twenty-five-year history, Manchester Traction was relatively free of trolley accidents and related personal injuries. In his definitive work, The Manchester Street Railway, O.R. Cummings mentions only three significant incidents. The first took place in 1912, when a trolley was at the end of the McGregorville - Derryfield Park line. Cummings says:

> ...It appears that Motorman Harold Leavitt set the air brakes on the car at Derryfield Park while he and Conductor Martin R. Sullivan stepped outside for a brief chat or a smoke. While they were standing some distance from the car it began to move, and rapidly gained momentum as it descended Derryfield Hill toward Elm Street. Narrowly missing a Beech Street car at the corner of Beech Street and left the rails as it tried to negotiate the curve onto Elm Street, plunging into the front of the E.M. Chase furniture store. Both the trolley and the store front were badly damaged, but fortunately there were no passengers in the car and no employees or patrons in the store.

The two other accidents occurred in 1924. The first of the two was when a B&M switch engine, used to shift or adjust tracks, hit a trolley. In Cummings' words:

> Newspaper reports of the incident indicate that a gateman at the crossing, not noticing the shifter, had raised the gates after a through train had passed. Operator Lewis Gilson was half way over the crossing when he noticed the shifter coming. He reversed the car and managed to get almost clear–but not quite. The vestibule of the trolley was demolished by the locomotive, but there were no injuries.

Clearing the wreckage from the Chase Building. (Courtesy of O.R. Cummings)

In reference to the second accident in 1924, Cummings continues:

> A few days later, on October 26, another one-man car, No. 120, left the rails at the corner of Hayward and Jewett Streets on the Valley Street line and overturned. Six persons were hospitalized but all were released after treatment for minor injuries.

Potential trolley wrecks were not the only danger with which early street car commuters had to deal. There was also the weather. The Daily Mirror and American featured a news story under the headline, "Spent the Night in a Trolley Car." Two passenger cars became stuck in snow drifts. Two snow plows and a sweeper, sent to rescue the trolleys, also became victims of the weather. It was decided to wait until the next day for further rescue attempts. The article summarizes the eventual rescue as follows:

> This morning another crew of men was sent out to their assistance and after working nearly all morning succeeded in getting through so that they could communicate with the bestranded passengers... and after coming within a few yards of the car they got out and climbing over a snowbank... they succeeded in reaching the car and found the passengers and the motorman and conductor enjoying themselves in a quiet snooze. They had worked nearly all night trying time and time again to gain headway but

without success. Several of the gentlemen passengers had started on foot early last evening for the city so that only five were left to enjoy the novel experience of being stuck in a snowdrift within two miles of the city hall for nearly twenty-four hours.

The reader should remember that the above incidents are the exception to a twenty-five-year record of excellent safety by Manchester Traction, Light and Power Co.

During this period, approximately half of the corporation's board of directors were from Boston, which was the location of Tucker, Anthony & Co., the firm's investment banking house. The other half of the board was located in Manchester. Among the long-term Manchester directors were R.G. Sullivan, William Parker Straw (the agent of the Amoskeag Manufacturing Co., who also was the grandson of Ezekiel Straw, the first president of the Manchester Horse Railroad), and J. Brodie Smith. Sullivan was the proprietor of the local cigar factory, which gained a national reputation for giving the country what it needed, which was Dexter, a good five-cent cigar. In addition, the factory produced 7-20-4 cigars, a quality ten-cent product.

J. Brodie Smith

J. Brodie Smith served as the general manager for the entire life of Manchester Traction, Light and Power Co. When that firm was merged into Public Service Co. of New Hampshire in 1926, he continued in that capacity for fourteen additional years. In addition to his role in bringing electricity to the state, Smith was a member of the Manchester Board of Water Commissioners and a trustee of the Elliot Hospital. When he passed away in 1947, the Reverend Martin Goslin, pastor of the Franklin Street Congregational Church, made the following observations in his eulogy after commenting on Smith's vocation and avocation with electricity:

> But in this hour it is well for us who are his friends, his fellow workers and his fellow townsmen, to recall his interest in an even greater and nobler power. Brodie Smith knew a source of energy far greater than that

developed by any dynamo - one more wondrous than the energy borne on waves of water. He knew the strength of man's noblest principles and values expressed in wholehearted, unselfish service to his fellow man.

For more than a score of years his interest and time have been devoted to our leading hospital. For years he has given of his time and strength and influence in the service of crippled children. Thirty years ago he led in the work of those afflicted with tuberculosis in our state. This human instinct ceased not on the frontier of physical health alone, but permeated his work with the Boy Scouts, his service as one of the founders of the Manchester Institute of Arts and Science, and our Historical society, and his constant labors in the oldest civic club of our city–the Rotary club.

Keene Square, 1908.

Dover outdoor substation, 1928.

Chapter 4

Electric Firms Across the State

The rest of the state was not waiting for Manchester to illuminate its communities and to transport its citizens. The actions of Manchester Traction, Light and Power Co. and its predecessors were paralleled in cities and towns in the seacoast and the mountains. From community to community it was a question of which arrived first, the electric light or the streetcar? Obviously, if it was the streetcar, it was a horse-drawn railroad. Generally, the less densely populated the area, the less likely a streetcar and the later the conversion from gas to electric street lighting.

Since there were well over 100 different firms throughout the state between the years 1890 and 1910, an examination of all these organizations is beyond the scope of this book. However, four different areas will be examined: the Exeter-Hampton area on New Hampshire's seacoast; the tri-city area of Dover-Rochester-Somersworth slightly north of Exeter and Hampton; the Keene area in the western end of the state; and the Berlin-Gorham area in the northern section of the state.

The most flamboyant character in the development of traction companies in New Hampshire was Wallace D. Lovell. Among his trolley companies were the Exeter, Hampton & Amesbury Street Railway and the Dover, Somersworth & Rochester Street Railway. While he played a major role in building or overbuilding these lines located in the eastern part of the state, he would soon lose control of all of the trolley companies in his empire.

At its peak the Exeter, Hampton & Amesbury Street Railway

System controlled 75.4 route miles of trolley lines. Exeter, the Rev-
olutionary capital of New Hampshire and the home of Phillips Exeter
Academy, at the time was the site of cotton textile manufacturing.
Hampton, located to Exeter's east, is one of the few New Hampshire
communities situated on the Atlantic Ocean. Amesbury is a neighboring Massachusetts community. The EH&A owned 20.7 miles
outright and leased an additional 54.7 miles from six other traction
companies. The company was formed in 1899 as a merger of the
Exeter Street Railway, the Hampton & Amesbury Street Railway and
the Rockingham Electric Co.

The Exeter Street Railroad, the earliest of these three firms, had
its origin ten years earlier when the New Hampshire legislature authorized the construction of an electric trolley system originating
from the Boston and Maine depot in Exeter heading east to a second
B&M depot in Hampton Village and continuing east to Hampton
Beach. With only 18 miles of coastline, New Hampshire boasted that
Hampton was the best natural beach north of Cape Cod. Since both
of the B&M stations were providing north-south traffic, the trolley
served as an excellent complement to the steam railroad for passengers wishing to vacation at the seashore. While the project appeared
to be a natural, there was difficulty raising the funds necessary for
the construction.

In 1897, Wallace D. Lovell acquired control of the franchise and
began the construction of trolley rails and a power plant located mid-
way between the two towns. At the same time, Lovell organized the
Rockingham Electric Co., which was to purchase electricity from the
Exeter Street Railway for distribution of electric service to the citizens
and municipalities of these two communities. This second corporation
was formed since railroads and trolleys were not permitted to sell
electric service directly to the public. In fact, the Board of Railroad
Commissioners were skeptical as to the legitimacy of Lovell's plan.
But ultimately they acquiesced. One of Rockingham Electric Co.'s
first customers was the town of Exeter. It paid just under $5,500 for
one year of street lighting.

The construction of the trolley line and power plant were completed on July 3, 1897. The fare to the beach from the Exeter Depot
was 15 cents. The fare from the Hampton Depot was 5 cents. In the

first year of operation there were over 550,000 passengers. Gross receipts were $29,000 with $24,100 in operating expenses and bond interest, leaving a tidy profit of $4,900.

Spurred on with the success of the first year of operation, the ambitious Lovell decided to organize a new line called the Hampton & Amesbury Street Railroad. The intention was to run a line from Hampton village to the Massachusetts border and to connect with the Haverhill & Amesbury Street Railroad, opening up northern Massachusetts with a direct trolley line to the beach. Lovell incorporated the Amesbury & Hampton Street Railway, a Massachusetts corporation, and completed the route to the Haverhill & Amesbury line. All of these projects were operational by July of 1899. As might be expected, this expansion in trolley miles required addition to both the moving stock and the power source.

In his treatise, "Trolleys to the Casino," O.R. Cummings makes the following observation on Lovell's business tactics:

> The operation of through routes, such as from Haverhill to Hampton Beach and from Newburyport to Hampton Beach, in cooperation with the Haverhill & Amesbury Railway was a goal of the EH&A management but the Haverhill & Amesbury wasn't willing to cooperate. From the point of view of its own interests, the H&A was justified in its stand for it was actively promoting Salisbury Beach [Massachusetts] as a summer resort and Hampton Beach was regarded as a dangerous competitor.
>
> But Promoter Lovell was a determined man and he was not above a little arm twisting to attain his ends. During September 1899, he announced plans to extend the Amesbury & Hampton from Amesbury to Haverhill... The Amesbury & Hampton, however, made no attempt to obtain state authorization for the extension–nor did it apply for franchises in any of the communities involved. But the mere threat of completion was enough for the Haverhill & Amesbury and early in January 1900, it joined the EH&A in inaugurating a through service between Newburyport and... Hampton Village.

A new corporation, the Exeter, Hampton & Amesbury acquired the assets of the E&H, the H&A and the Rockingham Electric Co. Since the A&H was a Massachusetts corporation, it could not be acquired outright, but it was controlled through a lease agreement.

To stimulate increased traffic to Hampton Beach, Lovell had the EH&A build a casino complete with bowling alleys, a pool hall, food stands, a dining room and a large function hall. Surrounding the casino were recreational fields and a bandstand. In subsequent years the casino would be expanded twice and a new 57-room hotel was constructed to the north side. In addition to stimulating demand for trolley traffic for a day at the beach, this complex increased the

Hampton trolleys in front of the Casino.

demand for electric lights. When the Casino and Ocean House Hotel boasted of a light in every room, many of the boarding houses and hotels in the area signed up with Rockingham Electric for this new service. Rockingham Electric Co. was authorized to increase its market beyond Exeter and Hampton, to include Hampton Falls and Seabrook.

These expansions did not squelch Lovell's desire for growth. He envisioned a trolley empire in southeastern New Hampshire and northeastern Massachusetts. He was provided financial backing from the New York Security & Trust Co. By 1901 he had organized five additional trolley lines including the Dover, Somersworth & Rochester Street Railway discussed below. These lines were incorporated into the EH&A System through lease agreements. In addition, he purchased the Portsmouth Gas, Electric Light & Power Corp. to provide additional electrical energy for the trolley system and for the

Rockingham County Light & Power Co. An additional $300,000 was spent to build a new generating station at the Portsmouth Facility.

Unfortunately, increased revenue did not grow proportionately with the increased overhead associated with the additional construction and acquisitions. The EH&A System was unable to meet its obligations with the New York bankers. The New York Security & Trust Co. took over Lovell's holdings. He stayed on for one year as a salaried manager to oversee the completion of the remaining lines. The overdeveloped lines did not prosper after the change in management. For the year ending June 30, 1903, the EH&S had a loss of $29,300 and additional losses of $78,900 on its leased lines. The following year losses were $10,200 and $72,200 respectfully. While the various Hampton Beach runs were profitable during the summer seasons, these profits were not sufficient to carry through winter operations.

The bonds of the EH&A were held by outside interests. In 1905, when the firm was unable to make its interest payments, the trolley line went into receivership. The court appointed Attorney Allen Hollis, president of the Concord Electric Co., to oversee the operations during the receivership. The various operating leases with the six other trolley lines were canceled and the accrued losses on these lines were written off. The operations continued as previously. Despite Hollis' best efforts, the system could not operate profitably. When the firm could not meet its November 1907 interest payment, the Superior Court ordered the property be sold at bankruptcy. All of the stockholders lost their investment. Ownership of the firm now was in the hands of the former bondholders which was reorganized under the Exeter Railway & Lighting Co. The new firm held all of the shares of the EH&A Trolley Line and all the shares of a new corporation entitled the Exeter & Hampton Electric Co. This entity assumed the responsibility of distributing electricity to residents and municipalities.

Following the reorganization, the trolley system met with modest success over the next eleven years. In September 1918, the company filed a petition for abandonment of the services with the New Hampshire Public Service Commission. After considerable delay, operations were taken over by the Town of Hampton, which ran the system as a municipal operation until 1926. While the EH&A Street

Railway ultimately fell victim to Henry Ford's idea of an affordable automobile, the Exeter & Hampton Electric Co. prospered in providing electric service to an increasing number of communities in the Hampton and Exeter area.

Hampton Beach.

Slightly north of Exeter and Hampton is the tri-city area of Dover, Somersworth and Rochester. All three cities were engaged in textile manufacturing. In the tri-city area the streetcar arrived almost simultaneously with the electric light. In 1882 a group of local businessmen provided sufficient electricity to a limited number of arc street lights. The company lasted approximately two years at which time its equipment was sold for junk. In 1882, the same year that the first arc lights illuminated Dover's streets, the Dover Horse Railroad began operations on 2.4 miles of track within Dover's city limits.

In 1887, H.W. Burgett, who was associated with the Thomson-Houston Co. a supplier of electric streetcar equipment out of Brookline, Massachusetts, organized the Dover Electric Co. This electric company contracted to provide the city with sixty-three electric lamps at an annual charge of $5,040. In 1890, the Dover Electric Co., now operating under the name Consolidated Light and Power Co. purchased the street railroad.

Consolidated Light and Power Co., under Burgett's direction, proceeded to build the Union Street Railway, a six-mile electrified line from Dover to Somersworth. At the same time that the rails were being laid for the electrified line, Burgett constructed an amusement park on Willard Pond, which was located at the midpoint of the new line. Burgett then converted the horse line within Dover to electricity and connected the tracks with the Union Street Railway.

After four years of operation, the line was in default and the property was taken over by the bondholders. The following year the firm's name was changed to the Union Electric Railway. The line was in drastic need of repairs and $100,000 of new funds were invested to rehabilitate the equipment, roadbeds and tracks.

In 1900, Wallace D. Lovell purchased the Union Electric Railway. About the same time he purchased the franchise for the Rochester Street Railroad, which never had built. Lovell then incorporated the Dover, Somersworth & Rochester Street Railway. He then merged into the new corporation the assets of the Union Electric Railway. By midyear 1901, he constructed an electrified line connecting with the Dover Somersworth line thereby uniting the three cities by trolleys. In November of the same year, ownership of the DS&R was transferred to New Hampshire Traction Co., Lovell's holding company. When New Hampshire Traction Co. went into bankruptcy in 1905, the DS&R was taken over by New Hampshire Electric Railways.

The bankruptcy of New Hampshire Traction Co. was a result of Lovell's merger mania and should not reflect on the soundness of the DS&R operation. Because of the interdependence of these three abutting cities and the lack of alternative transportation, this was one of the state's most successful traction operations. In 1924, in keeping with a more rational merger movement in electric utilities, New Hampshire Electric Railways was acquired by the Associated Gas and Electric Co. As a result of declining patronage, the trolleys were replaced with a bus system in 1926. Four years later, the DS&R, which by then was only a bus service, was sold to Leander Lynde, the company's superintendent since 1912.

On the western side of the state is the City of Keene. At the end of the nineteenth century, the community's economy was based on diverse manufacturing industries and later Keene became the site of one of the state's two teachers' colleges. In 1886, the Keene Gas Light Co. introduced the city to electricity when it installed an electric light generator at the gas works. The first year it had an arc street lighting contract and six commercial customers. Both the firm's capacity and number of electric customers grew to the point that in 1901 the firm's name was changed to Keene Gas & Electric Co.

In 1905, the Citizens Electric Co. was organized and began competing with KG&E. The new firm succeeded in making inroads into the market and was subsequently absorbed into Keene Gas & Electric Co. in 1908. The following year KG&E began servicing the abutting town of Winchester.

In 1911, KG&E formed a subsidiary corporation, Ashuelot Gas & Electric Co., to construct power lines from a hydroelectric plant on the Connecticut River to the Keene market. When the line was completed the following year, KG&E discontinued producing its own steam-generated electricity and entered into a ten-year contract to purchase its power needs from the Connecticut River Power Co.

Following the acquisition of this more economical source of power, KG&E experienced a period of both internal and external expansion. In reference to the former, it extended service to Spofford, Westmoreland and Chesterfield. In reference to the latter it purchased the Dublin Electric Co., the Marlboro Electric Light, Heat & Power Co. and the municipal electric plant in the town of Peterborough. Since these three acquisitions each had their own power plants, KG&E was back in the production of its own electricity.

In 1887, the year following the first arc lighting in the city of Keene, a group of local businessmen formed the Keene Street Railway Company. The firm was chartered by the state to "use horses or any other suitable form of motive power for the cars." The organization remained dormant until 1893 when it reorganized as the Keene Electric Railway. However, lack of funds and difficulty in granting local franchise agreements for the laying of tracks and the erection of power lines stalled the project. In 1900 Thomas T. Robinson of the Boston Industrial Co. agreed to construct the proposed line provided the local residents sold their shares of the Keene Street Railway Co. to him. While the original plan by the former owners was to purchase electricity from the Keene Gas Light Co., Robinson's firm decided to construct its own power station.

On September 10, 1900, regular service began in Keene and the neighboring community of Marlboro. The tracks ran a total distance of 6.3 miles. In 1903, a 2.1 mile line was added connecting the town of Swanzey.

In 1909, the company discontinued producing its own electricity and began purchasing from the Keene Gas & Electric Co., the renamed local utility company. Because of limited ridership, the firm experienced alternating periods of profits and losses. Rate hikes and fare zone changes were experimented with in an attempt to improve prosperity. In 1911, the Keene Electric Railway decided to take a page from its sister traction companies throughout the state. In an attempt to stimulate additional demand for ridership, it built a recreational facility adjacent to the trolley line. The company purchased land on Wilson Pond in Swanzey, where it constructed a dance hall and outdoor theater.

O.R. Cummings, in his "The Keene Electric Railway," quotes Arthur Parker referring to the difficulty of keeping tracks clear in the harsh New Hampshire winters:

> During the winter of 1919-20, we had several severe storms. Our snow plows were out for extended periods. This meant a big overload on the generators. Tending switchboards was part of my duties. In case of an overload... the plant is protected by circuit breakers. After a breaker is thrown, it has to be reset manually....
>
> During this period of storm, I was on duty continually for a period of 264 hours. How did I get any sleep? Here is how: I had a big rocking chair and tied a cord to the line switch and the chair post. When the breaker crashed out with a report like a rifle, I involuntarily jumped back, as I awoke from my cat nap. This threw out the line switch. It was only a matter of seconds to throw in the breakers, etc.–and then back to my fitful slumbers.

The harsh weather and limited ridership sent the firm into default on the interest to its mortgage bonds. In 1922, the stockholders lost all of their holdings and the bondholders' $80,000 bonds were replaced with a mixture of stocks and bonds. While the lowered capitalization did reduce fixed interest charges, the automobile increasingly was taking its toll. In 1926, the company switched to buses. At the end of

1929 the bus service was sold to the Cheshire Transportation Co.

While the trolley's use of electricity ended in 1926, the Keene Gas & Electric Co. continued to prosper.

Up north on the Androscoggin River lay the city of Berlin and the towns of Cascade and Gorham. All three communities' livelihoods relied on forestry. The river served a dual purpose to the pulp and lumber towns. In the pre-electric era, it provided the energy to run the saw mills and it also served as an economical means of transporting the fallen trees to the saw mills. The northernmost community, Berlin, was a leading pulp and paper producer. Its growth into a city was the product of the prosperity generated by its primary employer, the Berlin Paper Co. The company was founded and operated for many years by the Brown family. During World War I, the name was changed to the Brown Paper Co. in order to quell any possible bad feelings that might arise out of the German name Berlin.

Gorham, the southern most of the communities, was a noted lumber center. Cascade, located between Berlin and Gorham, was also a pulp and paper producer.

All three communities had their own power companies by the early 1890s; the Berlin Electric Co, the Gorham Electric Light Co. and the Cascade Electric Light & Power Co. For economy reasons the Gorham Electric Light Co. was acquired by the Cascade firm in 1895. The two remaining firms were acquired by Twin State Gas & Electric Co. in 1914.

The northern section of the state also had a trolley era. The Berlin Street Railway connected the town of Berlin with the town of Gorham. In 1899 a group of local residents incorporated the Berlin Street Railway. However, no construction was started until 1901 when Frank Ridon and Edward Gross purchased the franchise. The following year the company began running trolleys from Berlin to Gorham. The trolley system purchased its power from Cascade Light & Power Co. Like many of its fellow New Hampshire trolley systems, it purchased cars from Laconia Car Co., operating out of Laconia, New Hampshire. In addition to its regular runs between the two towns, the company operated special services to and from the plants of the Brown Co. during the commuting hours.

Following the lead of most other trolley systems, the company experimented with stimulating ridership by constructing a recreational facility. Cascade Park, located on the banks of the Androscoggin River, boasted a casino, athletic facilities and a natural dell functioning as an amphitheater. From its origin, the system had marginal profitability at best. On the other hand, the firm can claim to be the second to last system to shift to motorization. On December 1, 1938, the trolleys made their last run, leaving Manchester's trolley line as the only remaining active system.

Samuel Insull

Chapter 5

A Place in Samuel Insull's Empire

To understand how and why Public Service of New Hampshire Co. was organized in 1926, it is useful to travel back in
time to 1892 and halfway across the country to Chicago. That
year and location marked the beginning of Samuel Insull's,
career in public utilities, which would become synonymous
with public utility holding companies and stock pyramiding.

Insull emigrated from England in 1881 to become Thomas Alva
Edison's secretary. Over the years, Insull took on increasing responsibilities. He played a major role in the 1882 construction of Edison's
Pearl Street Station in New York City, the first major central power
facility in the country. The following year Insull was in charge of
the Thomas A. Edison Construction Department, building central
power stations throughout the country. In 1885, Insull's duties were
expanded to cover overseeing the newly built Edison Machine Works
in Schenectady. In 1889 when the Edison General Electric Co. was
formed by a merger of Edison's operation with the Sprague Co., Insull
was named chief operating officer.

Two schools of thought emerged as to the future of electrical
power. The Edison group believed in building its own central power
stations, equipped with Edison machinery. The Thomson-Houston
group believed that the future was in selling electrical equipment to
individual users or privately owned central stations. A merger was
proposed where Edison General Electric Co. would acquire the other
major producer of electrical equipment, the Thomson-Houston group,

thus resolving the future direction of power to the central station concept. However, the financial interests headed by J.P. Morgan, tipped the scales in the opposite direction. It is generally believed that the investment bankers preferred the more immediate profit from the sale of electrical equipment to the more long-run profits that would result from investments in power companies throughout the country.

A new firm, the General Electric Co., was formed through the union of Edison General Electric and Thomson-Houston. The name change was symbolic of Edison's loss of power. In the future, General Electric would move away from building central power stations and would concentrate on sales of its electrical producing machinery.

With the idea to make electricity available to everyone, Insull in 1892 packed his bags and headed west to Chicago to become president of the Chicago Edison Co. Some historians contend that Insull did not want to continue with General Electric since his role and influence would be reduced. Others hold that it was his belief in the future of central stations that prompted the move. Regardless of the reason, the situation that Insull found in Chicago was similar to what existed in New Hampshire at the time. There was duplication of effort with a host of competitive providers of electricity. Insull believed in the economies of scale in electric power generation. His goal was to create a monopoly to lower costs and prices and thus make electricity accessible to all households. He acquired local firms, often buying them for their customer base rather than their power facilities. When he requested a previously unheard of 5,000-kilowatt turbine from General Electric, he was refused until he agreed that it would be done as a joint-risk venture.

In 1907, Insull merged Chicago Edison and Commonwealth Electric, the two leading firms in the greater-Chicago market. The resulting company was sixty times larger than the firm he had taken over fifteen years earlier. At the local utility level, his theory on economies of scale in central power production was proved. He became a role model for public utility executives throughout the country and a champion by the customers because he provided low-cost electricity.

It is important to know that in 1898 in an address in front of the National Electric Light Association, Insull proposed that electric utility companies should seek to have themselves regulated by state commissions. He further proposed that a condition of franchising, or the exclusive right to operate in a given area, should be that a municipality would have the right to purchase at cost less depreciation the utility in question if it failed to provide satisfactory service. In effect, he wanted to insure that the monopoly position, which he advocated for economy in production, would not lead to price gouging of the customers or to inefficiency in operations.

Insull was a leader not just in the electric industry but in business in general, in employee relations and service to the community. He introduced a host of new employee compensation programs, including free medical benefits, profit-sharing and retirement plans. In addition, he encouraged stock ownership by employees by offering shares below the going market price. He also encouraged employee service to the community. He stated:

> I care not how good may be the franchise under which you operate... how able may be the management of your property... and how perfect your plants, unless you so conduct your business as to get the good will of the community in which you are working, you might just as well shut up shop and move away.

In 1902 at the request of certain bankers, Insull also took control of utility firms in the New Albany, Indiana, area. He placed his brother Martin in charge of these properties. Some eight years later he acquired a series of utility firms in Northern Illinois. As with his city projects, he generated improvements of services and lowering of prices through economies of scale. To facilitate raising funds for the development of these utilities, he formed the Middle West Utilities Co. Middle West, incorporated in 1912, was a holding company owning the stock of various operating utility companies. At the time, there was strong support for the holding company concept in utility industry. Arthur Stone Dewing, in his classic work The Financial Policy of Corporations, gave the following guarded evaluation of the advantages of public utility holding companies:

> It is presumed that the central organization gains a high degree of technical skill at a relatively low cost for the individual plant... is able to purchase material, equipment, and supplies more intelligently and at better terms... can deal more intelligently and farsightedly with the public authorities and the customers... [and] can secure the capital required for

expansion more easily and at cheaper rates of interest than the local organization.

From 1912, the year in which Middle West Utilities Co. was formed, until 1926, the year Public Service Co. of New Hampshire was incorporated, Samuel Insull developed a series of subsidiary holding companies. Insull appointed his brother Martin to head the major subsidiary corporations. In July 1925, Middle West Utilities Co. acquired control of Manchester Traction, Light and Power Co. for $150 per share plus a $2 dividend. The following year, Middle West transferred the

William Wyman and Martin Insull

ownership of the common stock to New England Public Service Co., one of its subsidiary holding companies. Public Service Co. of New Hampshire, was incorporated on August 16, 1926. Control of the new operating company was directly under New England Public Service Co. which was controlled by National Light, Heat and Power Co., which in turn was under Middle West Utilities Co. Under this arrangement, Martin Insull was the chairman of the board of Public Service Co, of New Hampshire. Walter S. Wyman, president of New England Public Service Co., served as president of PSNH. However local operations continued to be under the control of J. Brodie Smith, who had the title of vice-president and general manager.

In his 1976 work, *Fifty Years of Service: A History of Public Service Co. of New Hampshire,* Everett Sackett observed:

> To acquire some properties important to his Central Illinois Public Service Co. and its Indiana holdings, Insull had to buy all of the utility businesses owned by a New York investment banker, A.H. Brickmore. Brickmore had put his utilities into a holding company called National Light, Heat and Power Co. They included a company that served electricity in five towns in New Hampshire, four in Maine, two in Vermont, and one in upstate New York. Having acquired these properties, Insull's organization followed its usual practice of acquiring nearby properties in order to form an efficient system.

> Harry Wright, for forty-six years an employee of PSNH and the predecessor Keene Gas and Electric Co. recalls the circumstances of Middle West Utilities buying the Keene company.... One day a stranger came to the office saying he had a friend who would like to buy some stock in the company and asking Wright if he could get a financial report... He then had Wright arrange an appointment for him with [Treasurer and General Manager, Ralph D.] Smith. After the meeting Smith called Wright and accused him of trying to sell the company. The stranger came to see Wright again and said: "That man Smith is a funny fellow. He says he doesn't want to sell and I haven't even made him an offer." Other meetings were arranged, offers were made, and the company was sold. From Keene the buyer moved on to buy the Souhegan Valley Electric Co.

Chapter 6

Surviving the Early Years of the Great Depression

August 16, 1926, marked the beginning of Public Service Co. of New Hampshire as a separate legal entity distinct from Manchester Traction, Light and Power Co. It is interesting to contrast the two firms' advertisements in Manchester's City Directory for the years 1926 and 1927. In addition to the obvious name and management conversions, two other changes are noteworthy. The advertisement in the 1926 edition, reproduced in a previous chapter, emphasized the traction and amusement park. A 1927 advertisement, reproduced at the left, highlighted the company's new

Shoppers are attracted to PSNH window display.

An Electrifying History

corporate headquarters on the corner of Elm and Lowell Streets in Manchester. More important, emphasis was placed on appliances available at the company's showroom on the first floor of the new building. This provided two sources of revenue: profit from selling appliances; increased use of electricity. The copy read as follows:

> Power is furnished for all purposes, not only adding efficiency to industry, but also lightening household drudgery by running vacuum cleaners, washing machines, ironers, refrigerators, and all the modern appliances which are sold by the company.

Manchester Traction's assets were combined with those of three small utility companies scattered throughout the state: Keene Gas & Electric Co. and its subsidiary, Ashuelot Gas & Electric Co., Laconia Gas & Electric Co. and Souhegan Valley Electric Co., into the newly incorporated Public Service Co. of New Hampshire. Prior to the merger, the capital structure of Manchester Traction comprised $5.9 million in bonded debt and $5.0 million in common stock. The capital of the new corporation consisted of $8.8 million in bonded debt, $3.4 million in preferred stock and $5.0 million of common stock. The debt consisted of the former bonds issued by MTL&P and $3.2 million of a new issue of thirty-year PSNH bonds. All of the common stock was retained by New England Public Service Co.

The preferred stock was offered to the general investing public by Tucker, Anthony & Co., now headquartered in New York City, and Old Colony Corporation in Boston. Shares were sold to the public at $95 or $5 below their $100 par value. Preferred stock is a hybrid security, having some of the characteristics of both bonds and common stock. Like a bond, the security paid a fixed dollar amount, but as a stock, the disbursement was in the form of a dividend rather than interest. In the event of bankruptcy, the security would be paid after all debt but before any distribution to common stockholders. Unlike common stock, the preferred stock would not experience growth in dividends if the company prospered. In addition, the preferred stockholders did not have the right to vote for the directors who ran the company. This was entirely in the hands of the common stockholders, thereby ensuring control by Middle West through its subsidiary holding companies. However, if the company failed to pay the specified dividend in two quarters, the preferred stockholders would automatically gain

50

voting rights. This did not become an issue throughout the entire period that Public Service Co. of New Hampshire was controlled by Middle West, since the firm always had ample profits from which to pay the preferred dividends.

Martin J. Insull served as chairman of the board of directors. Walter S Wyman, president of the immediate holding company, served as the president. Local control was under the direction of J. Brodie Smith, vice president and general manager, and Avery R. Schiller, vice president in charge of operations. Schiller, who held an undergraduate and a graduate degree in electrical engineering from Harvard, had joined Manchester Traction in 1924, with twelve years experience in engineering and power companies. Schiller served with Insull and Wyman on the executive committee of the board.

The name, Public Service Co. of New Hampshire, was more an indication of future planned growth rather then actual status at the time of the amalgamation of the five original firms. Figures before and after the formation of PSNH indicate that Manchester Traction, which included service to Nashua and seventeen other communities in the Manchester-Nashua area, represented 78 percent of the revenue, 77 percent of kilowatt output, 61 percent of the gas output and 69 percent of the customers of the new corporation. However, it would not be long before PSNH would begin acquiring additional utility firms throughout the state.

In 1927, PSNH acquired Southern New Hampshire Hydro-Electric Corp. and Conway Electric Light & Power. The fact that these two companies were in opposite ends of the state is further indication of Public Service Co. of New Hampshire's goal to be a statewide utility company. In 1928, PSNH made three new acquisitions: Franklin Light and Power Co., Tilton Electric and Power Co. and Utility Power Co. The last of the three acquisitions together with a 1931 redevelopment which raised the dam some thirty feet, illustrates the synergistic effects of PSNH's purchases. Schiller comments on the process as follows:

> Prior to acquisition of this plant by Public Service, the owners could commit themselves to furnish no more power than the plant iterating itself as an isolated unit could produce during low-water periods. This naturally

limited the value and usefulness of the investment. When the station was interconnected with other plants of Public Service, deficiencies of low-water periods were made up from other power sources. Immediately upon interconnection, the identical power plant began producing at least three times as much electricity as it had under former ownership. Subsequently... the dam and pond at Ayers Island were enlarged, but the size of the water wheels and generators has remained. Today [1950] the plant turns out five or six times as much electricity as it did when operated as an isolated property.

To help meet the increased needs associated with its recent purchases and growing use of electricity by customers in existing markets, the company of retail utility companies purchased in 1929 the water power and steam-generating plant of Great Falls Manufacturing Co. located in Somersworth. Expansion continued in the 1930s. The utility company purchased the Eastman Falls Hydroelectric plant on the Pemigewasset River at Franklin from the Boston and Maine Railroad for $600,000 in 1930. That same year it merged four additional utility companies into its organization: Bethlehem Electric Co., Lisbon Light and Power Co., Compton Electric Light Co. and Freedom Electric Co.

Nineteen thirty-one was a year of both contraction and expansion. In September, PSNH discontinued operations of the Manchester and Nashua Street Railway. Traffic on all of the company's street railways was declining. The intercity service was shut down. That same year PSNH acquired the *Jacona*, a 20,000-kilowatt power ship from Central Maine Power Co, to provide needed additional power capacity. Central Maine Power Co., like PSNH, was controlled by Middle West Utilities Co. through New England Public Service Co.

The Jacona was originally launched in 1919 as a cargo steamer. In 1930, the vessel was purchased from the United States government for $5,000. The ship was sent to Newport News Shipbuilding and Dry Dock Co. where it went under a rather strange $1 million metamorphosis. The ship's main engine, boilers, foremast propeller and shaft were removed to make room for generating equipment. The final result was a portable 20,000-kilowatt plant. The oddity was that in the process of the transformation, the power plant lost it ability to power its own movement. While this was a planned result,

The Jacona

the anomaly made good reading in *Ripley's Believe It or Not.* The goal achieved was a power plant that could be moved by tug boats to various shoreline transmission locations within NEPSCo.'s holdings. To allow for eighteen-foot tides, steel towers were attached to the side of the ship and the dock. A loop in the cables between the two sets of towers and a dock allowed the ship to rise and fall with the tide.

The *Jacona's* first duty as a power plant was in November 1930 when it was towed to Bucksport, Maine. It was connected to the lines of the Central Maine Power Co. to supply power to a paper mill. Upon the completion of the Maine utility company's Wyman Dam at Bingham, whose capacity would provide the electric energy in that area, the ship was towed to Portsmouth the following April, where it provided power to the PSNH system until it was requisitioned in 1945 by the U.S. government for World War II.

In 1933, as a part of a corporate reorganization PSNH acquired Groveton Electric Light Co. and Lyman Falls Power Co. from its parent holding company, New England Public Service Co. To finance the expansion from 1926, the year of incorporation, to 1933, PSNH increased its bond debt from $8.8 million to $15.8 million. Simultaneously, it increased its preferred stock outstanding from $3.4 million to $9.4 million. A considerable amount of this increase in preferred stock was sold directly by the company to its customers. This practice was not particular to electric utilities or New Hampshire. The process was duplicated throughout the country. In his 1924 book, *The Common Sense of Money and Investments,* Merryle Stanley Rukeyser noted:

Customer ownership is temporarily turning gas fitters, telephone op-

Public Service Company with the addition of two floors, circa 1930.

erators and meter readers into stock salesmen. It is a scheme of banker-less finance... [reaching] individuals who never before bought securities and... permitting individuals of small means to buy securities on the partial payment plan....

Executives who have fostered the customer ownership movement assert that it has accomplished three main results. First it has taught the wider public the fundamentals of sound investment, thus adding stability to communities. Secondly, it has cultivated good will for utilities by enormously widening its circle of interested friends. Thirdly, it has provided a significant new source of capital.

It is interesting to contrast the growth in revenue and profit for the three years prior to the beginning of the Great Depression with the first five of the depression. For the years 1926 through 1929 revenue increased at an annual rate of 10.1 percent. Over the same time period profits grew at 7.3 percent. For the years 1929 through 1934 the annual growth rate in revenue slowed to 2.2 percent. Profits for the five years declined by 3.4 percent a year, far less than the economy as a whole.

Public Service Co. of New Hampshire's success in both of these periods can be attributed to three factors. The first was its strategy of acquiring small independent firms throughout the state. The second strategy was to construct high-voltage power lines connecting service areas, which allowed the most economical generating facilities to be used to their maximum capacities. The third strategy utilized was a three-pronged approach to increase usage. Expansion of rural service was made possible by the construction of rural lines. This program initiated in 1927 resulted in 290 new miles being completed by the end of 1931. The second approach was the establishment of a department for sales of electrical energy for manufacturing in 1928. To complement these first two expansions of usage, in 1929 the company established a home service department. The success of this final effort was demonstrated by the fact that from 1928 through 1931 the average residential usage per customer increased by 45 percent.

As the record above shows, the stock market crash and the Great Depression did not significantly hamper PSNH's profitability. To a great extent, utility companies were immune to the economic downturn because established customers did not want to lose the convenience of their electric lights or their labor-saving machines. In addition, because the utility companies were regulated industries, their profits were virtually guaranteed. Unfortunately or fortunately, depending on one's personal investments and political philosophy, the same could not be said for public utility holding companies. But that is subject matter for the next chapter.

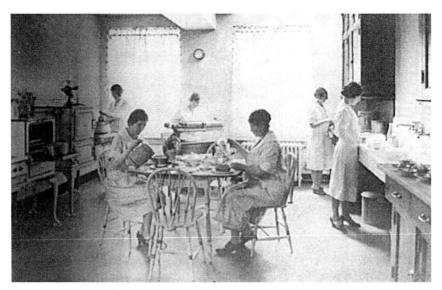

Employees in PSNH's Home Service Department, 1930.

Trolley drivers pose for a picture. John James McQueeney was the first of four generations to work for the utility company.

Chapter 7

The End of Public Utility Holding Companies

Opinions differ as to the ultimate cause of the decline in Insull's Middle West Utilities Co. that led to Public Service Co. of New Hampshire becoming an independent corporation. Forest McDonald, in his 1962 biography *Insull,* suggests that Samuel Insull's downfall was one of many unfortunate side effects of the Great Depression. N.R. Danielian disagrees. In his 1933 Atlantic Monthly article titled "From Insull to Injury," he condemns many of Insull's practices from the beginning of the holding company. Why did Insull fail? Danielian writes:

> The explanation here given has resolved itself showing, not so much why he failed, as how he kept himself from failing long before he did. Essentially there was no failure, because there was no success in his holding-company venture. *Insull only failed in hiding any longer the lack of success in his financing activities.* [Danielan's emphasis]

Both writers agree on the benefits that the various operating companies gained from Insull's operating management. Critic Danielian writes, "Most of the operating properties which Insull holding companies acquired were well managed before their entrance into the Insull domain, and still better run when they became a part of it." However, the two men had dramatic differences of opinions on the financial structure of the holding companies.

Insull's control of Middle West was never based on his personal ownership of the stock. Rather, his control was based on the proxy votes of stockholders satisfied with the current management. Biographer McDonald traces the origin of financial difficulties to the fall of 1928, when Insull discovered that there was an attempt by Cyrus S. Eaton, a Cleveland investment banker, to wrestle control of Middle West. In 1929, Insull formed two investment trusts, Insull Utilities Investments and Corporation Securities Co. of Chicago, in an attempt to acquire sufficient shares to maintain control of the holding company. The stock market in the late 1920s was suffering from its own "irrational exuberance" not unlike that found in the late 1990s. At that time, the hot new technology stock was "Radio", short for Radio Corporation of America. The market was also enchanted with the apparent growth opportunities associated with the leverage created by public utility holding companies. In all fairness to the 1920s market, at least it required the possibility of paying dividends.

As the bidding war for Middle West continued into August, the stock's price increased from $169 to $529. Simultaneously, the value of Insull Utilities Investments increased from its January opening of $25 to $150. In the process, Insull's personal wealth, on paper, went to $150 million. Since he had not been borrowing heavily, Insull survived the 1929 crash. McDonald's writes:

> As the fall of 1929 approached Insull's self-confidence was matched only by his strength and prestige. He demonstrated each when the great crash came in October. The first thing he did was to go to the rescue of his employees who were caught with marginal brokerage accounts by supporting, from his personal portfolio, whatever additional collateral they needed... With others, he began the construction of the great natural gas pipeline from the Texas panhandle to Chicago, a project that would cost around $80 million by the time it was completed, late in 1931... In January the City of Chicago itself stood facing bankruptcy, and Insull took on the task–immediately involving $50 to $100 million–of rescuing it and enabling it to pay its firemen, policemen and schoolteachers.

McDonald reports that in 1930 Eaton offered to sell his holdings of Middle West to Insull, with the warning that he could sell to a syndicate of New York investment bankers. Insull had greater concern with the potential of control falling into New York hands than remaining in the hands of Eaton. He resorted to borrowing to obtain Eaton's shares, at a total cost of $56 million. At this point, McDonald suggests a conspiracy theory where the New York investment bankers deliberately depressed the price of Insull's stocks to the point that he became insolvent.

N.R. Danielian presents a different interpretation of the causes leading to the fall of the Insull empire. He contends:

> The germs of decay had been implanted during the period of prosperity [prior to the 1929 crash.]... In the first place, large amounts of cash dividends were paid out, even though the companies possessed no net cash income after interest charges and expenses had been defrayed... Quantitatively the most important, and least comprehensible, method of wastage consisted of pegging transactions by the companies of their own or each other's securities on the stock exchange.

> The wisdom of an investment depends upon the nature of the business which is purchased, the management under which it is run, and the price at which the acquisition is made.

In reference to the operating management, Danielian gives Insull top grades. As to the price at which the acquisitions were made, however, Danielian writes, "In the choice of investments, and in the price paid for them, Insull was indiscriminate, even extravagant." Danielian then tells of a conversation with a former owner-operator of a New England utility company in which Danielian asked why he had sold his company to Insull. "He retorted: 'What in hell would you do if someone came along and offered you three times as much as your company was ever worth?'" Danielian then continues:

> Having paid high prices, having invested in questionable enterprises... Often investments were simply reevaluated at a higher figure, or, what amounts to the same thing, they were shuffled back and forth between sub-holding companies at continually rising values, resulting in an increasing asset value of the top holding company's investments.

Danielian contends that the efforts to inflate the value of the holding companies were not limited to asset assessment but also addressed the question of revenues and profits.

> The window dressing of the income account by which this condition was hidden from the outside world was achieved in several ways. [First,] insufficient provision was made for depreciation of operating-company properties. [Second,] the greatest source of cash was in ... sales of stocks and bonds. [Third, when intercorporate sales of assets were made at increased values,] the difference between the ledger value on the books of the "selling" company and the "sale" price paid by an affiliated or subsidiary company was entered as income and made available for dividend

disbursement. Finally, stock dividends by subsidiaries, which were often declared with little justification in actual earnings, were taken up by the higher holding companies into their income accounts at market value, and were made the basis of cash dividend payments.

Economist Arthur Stone Dewing's views on the motivations involved with corporate expansions provides an opinion somewhere between those of McDonald and Danielian. This analysis, authored in 1919, prior to Insull's downfall, very well could have been written with Insull in mind.

> Four main motives have led men to expand business enterprises. On the whole they are not economic, but rather psychological ... The most powerful motive that leads a man to expand a business is the illusion of valuing himself in terms of his setting. The bigger the business, the bigger the man.... The second motive, less significant... is the creative impulse.... [S]omewhere in the mental structure of all of us lies the impulse to build, to see our ideas form in material results.... The third motive is the economic. My own observation is that the vast majority of business men who plan enlargements, consolidations, and expansions of their business are not actuated primarily by the impulse to make more money, although they unquestionably place this motive uppermost when they need to present plans for enlargements to directors and stockholders.... The fourth motive is the satisfaction in taking speculative chances.... A successful business manager is invariably a man of imagination. Invariably the man of imagination revels in uncertainties.... All men enjoy the game they think they can play.

In April 1931, Insull traveled to New York in an attempt to gain new financing. It was decided by the creditor not to lend any further money to Middle West forcing the holding company into receivership. Insull's two investment trusts quickly followed. Two months later, Insull was asked to resign from Commonwealth Edison, the Chicago operating company he had run since 1892. Shortly thereafter, Insull said he was traveling to Europe for a much needed vacation. The vacation turned into a search for refuge from prosecution. His travels included France, Greece and Turkey. While in Istanbul, he was arrested and extradited. He returned to the United States. In October he was tried on mail fraud charges. The following March he was tried on embezzlement charges. In both trials, he was found innocent of any illegal activity. However in the court of public opinion, his reputation was permanently blemished.

As for Public Service Co. of New Hampshire, it matters little which view of history is more correct. As a result of the stock market crash and the subsequent fall of the Insull empire, Middle West Utilities Co. lost control of all of its New England operating companies, including Public Service Co. of New Hampshire. Middle West's control of these companies was through a subsidiary holding company, New England Public Service Co. Insull had used Middle West's shares in New England Public Service Co. as collateral for a loan in which he subsequently defaulted.

Samuel Insull is released from jail.
(Brown Brothers photo)

Walter S. Wyman

Walter S. Wyman, president of New England Public Service Co., purchased the company from the banks to which Insull defaulted. NEPSCo. still controlled PSNH, in addition to two primarily Maine utilities, Central Maine Power Co. and Cumberland County Power and Light Co., two primarily Vermont utilities, Central Vermont Public Service Corp. and Twin State Gas and Electric Co., and two smaller companies. The loss in confidence in the holding company concept prompted legislation in 1933 that ultimately resulted in PSNH and similar operating companies becoming independent corporations.

Early transmission station, about 1930.

Chapter 8

Emerging from the Great Depression

Perhaps the darkest hour in the Great Depression for the New Hampshire economy was when the Amoskeag Manufacturing Company declared bankruptcy. Amoskeag had survived for more than 100 years. It was incorporated in 1831. Over the years its Manchester mills gained an international reputation for the quality of their textile products. In the last decade of the nineteenth century, the directors noted the increased competition from the lower labor cost in the South. Over the next three decades, many New England textile firms directed their future expansion in the South. Others simply closed their New England plants. Amoskeag, however, declared that it always was and would remain a New Hampshire firm. It had two significant expansions, one in the 1886 and the second in 1909.

Following the high profits associated with World War I, Amoskeag began operating at a loss. In 1922 the company tried to regain its competitive edge by lowering wage rates to bring it in line with the South. A nine-month strike followed and the original rate was restored. Following the strike, employment averaged far below its former level as the firm reduced production to minimize losses. Conditions worsened when the nation fell into the Great Depression.

For a brief time, the depression brought new hope to Amoskeag because of the workers need for employment. One of the programs proposed by President Franklin Delano Roosevelt in 1933 was the National Recovery Program. The program aimed to end the downward spiral in prices and wages by having firms agree to maintain a uniform price and pay a uniform wage. Uniform prices would be on a national level. What was yet to be determined was whether the uniform wage rate would be a national level, or whether the South should be able to pay its labor at a lower wage rate. Frederic C. Dumaine, a lifetime Republican but supporter of Roosevelt's programs, was the treasurer, or chief executive officer, of Amoskeag at the time. On June 28, 1933, he went to Washington to speak in favor of the NRA. A portion of his comments in front of National Recovery Hearings include:

> It is not my purpose to burden you with a mess of figures or argue at length details upon which you have spent untold hours... I do, however, want to say the industry's condition as it is and as it has been for years is due to reckless and unbusinesslike methods of distribution. Ruthless competition has forced wage rates out of all reason and carried living conditions of workers below American standards. Prevailing wages have not increased consumption or brought benefits equaling the oppression it has caused the workers.

> It's high time an industry incapable of intelligently managing its affairs should be forced to accept outside control... I'm heartily in accord with the principle here being considered and differ only with certain details of the measures execution.... Unless there is rigid control of machinery output and expansions, the whole object of this Act is defeated.

> Representing a concern existing for a century and employing some 8,000 workers [down from the original 17,000], I solemnly protest the proposed differential in wages by districts. The industry is located in a common country, there should be no differences... between states or communities. Workers and owners of one section should not be obliged to carry handicaps and when their products reach a common market they should carry a substantially equal cost and bring an equal price for quality.... With no desire to irritate our very good southern friends, *I'm constrained to say no fair person will object to a code providing equally for the workers, the owner and the consumer* [Author's emphasis]... If you, sir, and your assistants can define and lay down a code of procedure whereby all concerned will receive like consideration you will have rendered a great service to your fellow-countrymen and supported our great leader in his supreme effort for the commonweal.

While Dumaine received personal thanks from President Roosevelt for endorsing the program, the South won the political battle and a difference in wages was established. In retrospect, this decision was not of great significance since the U.S. Supreme Court soon ruled the National Recovery Act unconstitutional.

As might be expected conditions did not improve. In the Fall of 1935 the mills were closed. On December 24, 1935, the firm filed for bankruptcy reorganization. Critical to a successful reorganization were: a) the workers must accept a rate equal to that in the South, and b) a majority of bond holders needed to accept preferred stocks in exchange for their bonds, which were in default. The situation was complicated by a March flood that caused over $2.5 million in damages to the mills. While Amoskeag did get the consent of labor for a wage equal to that in the South, too few of the bondholders agreed to go along with the reorganization. Amoskeag withdrew its reorganization plan and the bankruptcy preceded. At this point three bankruptcy trustees were appointed by the court. They were Dumaine, Amoskeag Manufacturing Co.'s treasurer, William Parker Straw, the third generation of former agents of the mills, and Joseph Carney of the U.S. government's Reconstruction Finance Committee.

The original liquidation plan called for an auction of the mills and equipment. It was anticipated that there would be a substantial number of bidders for the equipment from the South and overseas. While this would probably maximize the proceeds from the liquidation, it would make the reopening of Manchester's mills more difficult once the equipment was removed. With this in mind, a group of Manchester

Lineman of the 1940s.

Fathoming the flood at Amoskeag.

businessmen formed a new corporation, Amoskeag Industries, hoping to purchase the mill property in its entirety. Three key individuals in this attempt were William Parker Straw, the former Amoskeag agent, Arthur Moreau, a former mayor of Manchester, and Avery R. Schiller, vice-president in charge of operations at Public Service Co. of New Hampshire.

In his 1997 book, *Dumaine's Amoskeag: Let the Record Speak*, Arthur Kenison attributes the inevitable closing of the Amoskeag Manufacturing Co. to the dramatic difference between New England and Southern labor costs. He presents documents of the company that attribute the decision by the company to withdraw its reorganization proposal as a result of:

> ...the damage done by the flood since the filing of said Plan, and greatly accelerated expenditure from its quick assets for repairs and... on account of the further shrinkage of quick assets which would result from... a disappointing large number of bondholders, and the failure of more than one half in amount of New Hampshire bondholders to leave their money in the business.

Kenison further contends that, as a bankruptcy trustee, Dumaine played a major role in facilitating the purchase of the entire mill property by Manchester locals, to minimize the impact of the bankruptcy on Manchester.

William Parker Straw, who had been fired by Dumaine in 1929 in hopes that a change in the local operations management might rejuvenate the ailing firm, presents an alternative interpretation of the situation. In a pamphlet published by the American Branch of the Newcomen Society of England, Straw writes:

> It would be fruitless to speculate upon the causes of its downfall. Perhaps Southern competition was one reason; perhaps mills and machinery were not sufficiently modernized; perhaps the sales policy was at fault; perhaps some blame could be attached to the management. Every piece of its machinery, all its equipment, all its buildings, all its land and houses and tenements throughout the city, together with its great water power and steam plants, were destined for the auction block.

In reference to the purchase of the mill property by Amoskeag Industries, Straw says:

> In 1936, when things were the bleakest, a group of Manchester's citizens, more venturesome, more courageous and more enterprising than others, determined to work out some plan to keep industry in the city and circumvent the auction block which would have meant complete disaster to the whole community.

> After a series of negotiations, the court, or the referee in bankruptcy into whose arms the old Amoskeag had fallen, agreed to sell the whole property, lock, stock, and barrel, for $5,000,000 in cash, so the problem became how to raise the five million. A canvass of Manchester people netted $560,000, subscribed for stock of the new company, the Public Service Co. agreed to buy the water power and the steam plant at the Northern Division for $2,250,000, and the Savings Banks of the city agreed to loan on mortgage the balance needed. It was a day of great jubilation when in October 1936 the deal finally went through! The city had a new lease on life! *It had a chance to come back!*

It matters little to the history of Public Service Co. of New Hampshire as to which interpretation is accepted. John Pierpont Morgan, the late nineteenth and early twentieth century financier, is often quoted as saying, "There are two reasons why an individual does something, a good reason and the real reason." The quip is not as cynical as it

Dover, New Hampshire, outdoor substation.

first appears when used to explain the actions of business leaders. Since corporate directors are trustees of stockholders' wealth, they cannot arbitrarily abuse their trusteeship for the public good. They can only take on public projects, when the projects parallel the best interests of the stockholders the directors represent. While the actions taken by Dumaine and the other directors allowing the newly founded Amoskeag Industries to acquire the mill property on a noncompetitive basis served the Manchester community, it also insured that Amoskeag Manufacturing Co. would receive sufficient capital to pay off all debts and leave a small amount for equity holders. The local businessmen who formed Amoskeag Industries and the local banks that provided the necessary financing for the good reason of keeping all equipment in Manchester thereby facilitating the eventual rehiring of the local labor force, were conscious of the fact that the price paid was a mere fraction of the replacement cost of the assets acquired.

In a similar manner, Public Service Co. of New Hampshire could fulfill its social contribution to the local community (the good reason) while acquiring additional energy sources at a most favorable price (the real reason). In addition to the $2.25 million that it paid for Amoskeag's water rights and its hydroelectric and steam generators, PSNH also contributed $100,000 of the $560,000 equity investment in Amoskeag Industries. The purchase of Amoskeag's 16,000-kilowatt hydroelectric power plant increased Public Service Co.'s capacity by 19 percent. The $100,000 investment in Amoskeag Industries ensured the goodwill of the community.

PSNH's acquisitions in the second half of the Great Depression were not limited to the Amoskeag property. In a 1937 intercorporate transaction, it acquired the Swan Falls Co. from its parent corporation, New England Public Service Co. That same year, the Manchester Street Railway, formerly held as a wholly-owned subsidiary, was merged into PSNH.

From 1935 to 1939, PSNH saw its customer base grow by 13 percent to over 71,500 residential, rural, commercial and industrial users of electricity. The number of communities served grew from 115 to 165. Kilowatt-hour sales grew by 40 percent to over 266 million. Electric generating capacity increased by an even more impressive 50 percent to 126,444 kilowatts. Electric revenue increased by 32 percent to over $5.8 million. To finance the growing demand for electricity, the firm sold about $3 million in bonds and a similar amount of stock. Public Service Co. of New Hampshire, like most medium to large electric operating companies, weathered the financial storm of the Great Depression. As the previous chapter illustrates, the same was not true for most public utility holding companies.

Throughout the state, trolley tracks were being removed or abandoned.

Cornelius James McQueeney, the second of four generations who worked for PSNH, poses with one of Public Service Company's new buses.

Chapter 9

A Decade of Transition

A decade of big change was ahead for PSNH in which both internal and external changes in the operations, management and ownership of the company would evolve. The most significant change in the method of operation was the replacement of the trolley system with buses. Internal changes included Avery Schiller replacing Brodie Smith as the operating head of the organization. The external change in ownership, which had begun in 1931 when Middle West Utilities Co. lost control of PSNH, went one step further when common stock was offered to the general public in 1946. Eventually in the 1950s, Public Service Co. of New Hampshire would become an independent corporation. During the 1940s, the company also experienced substantial growth in revenue as a result of the war and postwar expansion.

In 1938, PSNH began substituting buses for trolley routes. The first route replaced was the Goffstown run servicing the northwest section of the city. Trolley service was operating at a time disadvantage against Notre Dame Bus Line because it had to operate on tracks that only crossed the river on the bridge at the south end of the city. In 1939, the company filed a petition with the New Hampshire Public Service Commission for the authority to completely replace trolleys with buses. In a 1973 history of Manchester bus service, Loring M. Lawrence wrote:

> The relevant facts of the case, presented at the hearing on September 21, were that patronage had declined 70 per cent from 11.9 million passengers in 1921 to 3.5 million in 1938, that rehabilitation of the streetcar

system would require $200,000 for new cars and $300,000 for track and roadbed, and that the conversion to busses would cost only $360,000... Car fares would remain at 10 cents. PSC approval was granted on January 31, 1940....

In addition to the trolleys, another Manchester institution would pass from the scene: Notre Dame Bus Line. [That firm experienced declining traffic since many of their patrons] chose to walk a block or two to the inbound [PSNH] Goffstown bus to secure a transfer and thereby save a second ten-cent fare in town... Notre Dame elected to sell out to Public Service....

The new routes were announced to the public by full-page newspaper advertising, and the conversion was made effective May 26, 1940. Late on Saturday evening the last six trolleys carried their passengers directly into the Traction Street car barn, accompanied by considerable cheering and clanging of bells. Buses got off to a grand start on Sunday morning, and hundreds of people spent the afternoon joyriding.

The new transportation system was an immediate success. In the first year of operation, revenue climbed 11 percent. A deficit was replaced with a $13,500 profit. The following year revenue increased 31 percent to 5.6 million passengers. By 1945, the number increased to 13 million, higher than any time in trolley history.

Public Service Co. of New Hampshire continued its absorption of independent utility companies when in October 1940 it purchased New Hampshire Gas and Electric Co. that provided retail service in the towns of Danbury and Hollis. Such acquisitions gave the state's leading electric company a presence in natural gas utilities. On the last day of the same year, PSNH acquired the Danbury Light and Power Co., which serviced the communities of Danbury and Grafton.

From its origin as Manchester Traction, Light and Power, the chairmanship and presidency were controlled by Tucker, Anthony and Co., the investment banking firm. When the utility was reorganized under the control of Middle West Utility Co., the chairman of PSNH was Middle West Vice President Martin Insull. Middle West Utility Co. controlled PSNH through an intermediate corporation, New England Public Service Co. The presidency of Public Service Co. of New Hampshire was held by New England Public Service Co.'s president Walter S. Wyman. When NEPSCo. emerged from the Insull bankrupt-

Avery R. Schiller

cies as an independent organization, it continued to control PSNH. Wyman retained the presidency of both corporations.

However, from the 1901 origin through 1940, the local operation was under the control of J. Brodie Smith, who held the title of vice president and general manager. In 1941, Smith stepped down from this position. While he retained his position as a corporate director and the title of Vice-President, the role of general manager was taken over by Avery R. Schiller. Schiller, a native of Spokane, Washington, earned degrees in electrical engineering from Harvard. He began his professional career with Boston-based Stone and Webster Management Associates. From there he moved to Connecticut Power Co. and then Adirondack Electric Power Co. In 1924 he came to Manchester as Assistant to the President of Manchester Traction, Light and Power Co. When the 1926 reorganization to Public Service Co. of New Hampshire occurred, Schiller was named Vice-President in Charge of Operations. It was Schiller who played a major role in PSNH's acquisition of Amoskeag's power plants. Schiller was elevated to vice president and general manager when Smith went into semi-retirement in 1941.

The following year, Schiller became president and general manager. This was the first time in the forty-one year history of MT, L&P and PSNH that the position of president was held by an internal officer of the company rather than by an officer of the controlling financial organization. While New England Public Service Co. would continue to maintain financial control over PSNH throughout the decade, this move was indicative of its eventual emerging as an independent corporation.

Control of the organization was effected by maintaining complete ownership of the common stock. Both Manchester Traction, Light and Power Co. and Public Service Co. of New Hampshire sold preferred stock to the general public. However, owning this stock did not give voting rights, that is, the ability to participate in the election of the directors of the corporation, unless the company failed to pay the preferred dividends. At that point each preferred share would have a vote equal to each share of common. This apparent ability to vote if the dividends were in default was ineffective in gaining any real power. The total number of preferred shares outstanding was always fewer then the number of common shares outstanding. Since all of the common shares were owned by the parent corporation, absolute control was guaranteed.

The reader should not assume that this corporate structure was an attempt to take advantage of the preferred shareholders. When individuals purchased stock, they were aware of their status. While they had no effective vote, they had prior claim to dividends, and in case of bankruptcy, prior claim to the firm's assets. More important, the preferred dividends were always paid. Also, it is interesting to note that under New England Public Service Co.'s control fourteen of the sixteen PSNH directors were New Hampshire individuals representing the various sections of the state serviced by the company. It appears that NEPSCo looked upon its ownership of PSNH as a financial investment. It was content to let the firm act independently as long as it continued to be run effectively.

However this total control by NEPSCo. began to erode in 1940 based on the Securities and Exchange Commission proceedings against the company under the Public Utilities Holding Company Act. The SEC found that for the five-year period 1935 through 1939 the NEPSCo.'s annual income, which consisted primarily of common stock dividends from its subsidiary operating companies, averaged a shortfall of $1.9 million in meeting the company's preferred dividend requirements. The SEC further held that if all the income available to common stock had been transferred to the parent company, the annual shortfall would average over $500,000. At the same time control of NEPSCo. was still in the hands of the common stockholders. In effect the SEC found that the firm belongs to the preferred stockholders. In light of these findings, in 1941 the SEC provided the company with the choice of either a one-stock plan of reorganization or the liquidation of the company to the benefit of the preferred shareholders.

That same year, New England Public Service Co. submitted a proposal for liquidation under which Cumberland County would be merged into Central Maine Power. PSNH would acquire the New Hampshire assets of Twin State Gas and Electric with Central Vermont acquiring the Vermont assets of Twin State. The plan called for the distribution of the shares of these three remaining utility companies to the shareholders of NEPSCo. Ownership of New England Industries, Inc., a subsidiary holding company controlling paper and textile mills would remain with NEPSCo. It was not until twelve years later in 1953, that final agreement as to the proportional distribution between the various classes of preferred and common stock was agreed upon and received SEC approval. In the end, the plan called for the sale of the assets of New England Industries, Inc. with the cash being distributed along with the share of the three utility companies to the shareholders of NEPSCo.

In accordance with the liquidation plan of NEPSCo, on December 28, 1943, the New Hampshire properties of Twin State Gas and Electric Co. were transferred to PSNH. The acquisitions in the first half of the decade increased the total number of communities serviced from 165 to 170. This external acquisition was far outweighed by a 37 percent increase in electric customers within the 165 districts. Even more impressive were the growth rates in kilowatt hours, 42 percent, and dollar revenue, 44 percent, as the country used a portion of its increased income associated with the wartime economy to purchase additional electric appliances.

Actual ownership of PSNH took a dramatic change in May of 1946 when the company made a public offering of common stock for the first time. Additional shares were sold to the public in 1948 and 1949. By the end of the decade, there were 5,966 individual common stockholders. While New England Public Service Co. still owned slightly more than half of the stock and maintained controlling interest, PSNH was on its way to becoming an independent corporation. These stock issues were used to finance the purchase and construction of additional plants increasing capacity by 85,000 kilowatts.

Prior to public ownership of its common stock, Public Service Co. of New Hampshire's annual reports were limited to financial data. Public bond and preferred stock investors anticipated fixed returns and obtained the necessary financial evaluations from investment rating agencies such as Standard and Poors or Moodys. Since all of the common stock was owned by NEPSCo., which had an inherent understanding of the scope of the business, all that was necessary were formal accounting statements. That all changed when common stock was issued to the general investing public. In addition to providing the necessary financial data and future investment plans of the company, the reports addressed issues of public and company concerns. Under Schiller's leadership, the annual reports treated such issues as economy in production associated with scale and the resulting need for regulation, the requirement of a reasonable return to capital, the obligation to reward a dedicated labor force, the company's obligation to the community, and the need to preserve the free enterprise system from the threats of socialism associated with movements towards public ownership of utilities

In March 1945, the U.S. government had requisitioned PSNH's *Jacona*, a 20,000-kilowatt floating power plant, for military purposes. However, some 20 months later in November 1946, Public Service Co. of New Hampshire purchased from the government in a postwar liquidation of excess military facilities, the *Resistance*, a 30,000-kilowatt floating power plant. This net increase of 10,000-kilowatt capacity fell far short of supplying the total growth in energy requirements in the 1940s.

Public Service Co. of New Hampshire purchased a small hydro-electric plant from George H. Jones in 1946. However, since this plant had formerly been leased by PSNH, the purchase did nothing to increase capacity. In 1948 the company completed a 15,000-kilowatt hydroelectric plant in the northern portion of the state. The Berlin, New Hampshire, plant was called the Smith in honor of J. Brodie Smith, who had passed away the prior year. In 1949, PSNH put into service a new mercury steam plant. This plant, located in Portsmouth, New Hampshire, which had a registered capacity of 40,000 kilowatts, was named after Avery R. Schiller.

In a simplification maneuver, Public Service Co. of New Hampshire sold all of its gas property to Gas Services, Inc. in 1946. PSNH and its predecessor corporation, Manchester Traction, Light and Power, had been in the gas business since the amalgamation of Nashua Light, Heat & Power Co. This acquisition, like PSNH's

1943 purchase of Twin State Gas and Electric Co., was the result of purchasing an electric company that also provided gas service. Gas was never a major portion of PSNH's total business. In the last full year of operation prior to the sale, gas amounted to four percent of the firm's total revenue.

During the last half of the 1940s, Public Service Co. of New Hampshire made three additional acquisitions of retail electric utilities. In 1945 it purchased the electric distribution system of Wonalancet Electric Co., which operated in Tamworth, New Hampshire. That same year PSNH acquired the Wakefield Power Co. The final purchase took place in 1948 when PSNH bought the electric distribution system owned by the Town of Hancock, New Hampshire.

The Hancock purchase is interesting inasmuch as it represented the purchase of a municipal system. There was considerable interest within the country with the concept of having all utilities state run. Todd M. Bohan, Ph.D., a former economist with the New Hampshire Public Utilities Commission and at the time of this printing with Unitil Service Corp., New Hampshire's second leading provider of retail electricity, presents the following background with which to address the question of public or private ownership:

> Attempts to explain the regulation of utilities focus on two areas: the provision of commodity that is *affected with the public interest* and the provision of a commodity that is supplied under conditions of *natural monopoly*. While one could make the case that most of the goods and services we consumer are goods and services that are *affected with the public interest,* public policy has typically limited its regulation, in this regulatory fashion we know to utilities. If that is the case there must be some other reason why utilities are regulated in the manner they have been. The answer seems to be that utilities, by their definition, operate under conditions of *natural monopoly.* This means that for reasons of reasons of efficiency, it is better to have one provider of the particular service in a geographic area verses a number of providers competing for business.
>
> Once the argument is made that the commodity being provided is being done so under conditions of *natural monopoly* the next question is how to allow the natural monopoly to operate. The two typical forms are a municipality or a regulated utility. A municipality results in the local government controlling the ownership and operations. A regulated utility provides the good or service, however, the utility is regulated by state

and federal commissions that govern what the utility can and cannot do, particularly setting limits on the prices which the utility can charge its customers.

The interest in public ownership of utilities preceded the designation of electric service as a utility. One of the early advocates of the concept was Richard T. Ely. Because electricity was in its infancy, most of his examples were in reference to railroads and trolleys. In *Socialism and Social Reform,* he wrote:

> The socialization of natural monopolies is a prerequisite for the problems of the present time connected with monopoly... [Natural monopolies] main characteristics are three: They occupy peculiarly desirable spots or lines of land; second, the service or commodity which they supply is furnished in connection with the plant itself; and, in the third place, it is possible to increase the supply of the service or commodity indefinitely, without proportionate increase in cost....

> The fact that particular desirable spots or lines of land are exclusive, gives a business an advantage. If the spots or lines of land are exclusive, of course that establishes a monopoly in itself... Streetcar lines, however, very often occupy what we may call exclusive lines of land, as in ordinary streets we cannot well have more than two tracks... The flower of one city may compete with the flower of another city, but the streetcar service of a city must be used in connection with the streetcar plant... The third characteristic, however, is the one of chief importance, for it includes, by implication, the other two. As the business increases in extent, the cost of the service or commodity decreases, consequently there is always an inducement held out to carry on the business as one undivided whole. If two competing companies are furnishing services or commodities of the kind mentioned... It is found that sooner or later attempted competition always gives way to combinations and consolidations.

> The socialization of monopoly will lead to better utilization of productive forces... Another advantage... is the utilization of existing inventions and industrial improvements. Private monopoly is opposed to improvements, because they involve additional outlays... The distribution of wealth would also be improved by socialization of monopoly... [Municipal monopolies could] be managed with reference to the greatest good of the greatest number. A special consideration could be shown to those who require help. The working-woman who, in cities, trudges to and from her work because she cannot pay a five cent streetcar fare, of which two cents represent economic surplus, could frequently ride instead of walk,

A 345 KV transmission line is installed across the Connecticut River between Hinsdale, New Hampshire and Vernon, Vermont, about 1950.

if the fare were reduced to three cents.

Based on the apparent success of the Tennessee Valley Authority in the Great Depression, and subsequent growth in public ownership in the states of Nebraska, Arizona and Washington there was increasing interest in the movement. A 1949 Fortune article titled "TVA Was Only the Beginning" warned:

> Indeed the outlook for private power in the entire Pacific Northwest is not encouraging. That region is growing rapidly and suffering from an acute power shortage. And the plain fact is that because of federal activities the private companies can do little to alleviate the shortage. No one is going to put money into facilities for high-cost electricity when underpriced federal power is or may become available.

One need only substitute "the retail price is regulated and the wholesale price is deregulated," for "underpriced federal power is or may become available," to read as if it came from a 2001 article on conditions in California. The Fortune article went on to state:

> Unfortunately, the vaulted "cheapness" of public power is a myth... because public power is not cheap but subsidized. Since 1933, the government has encouraged the widespread use of electricity by making it available at low rates regardless of cost... At best, all that the government can do is save the consumer the difference between its own bond rate and the 6 to 7 per cent rate of return allowed private companies. Any additional savings seemingly reflected in low public power rates is purely illusory.

The article then goes on to point out that federal and municipal utilities are not subject to taxes, resulting in the average utility user to have his electric rate savings offset by an increased tax burden.

In a 1951 letter to the shareholders, customers and employees of Public Service Co. of New Hampshire, Avery Schiller expressed his concern in this area:

> Public Service Co. of New Hampshire is a business managed electric utility... Each year it now pays in taxes more than it pays in dividends... By the exercise of proper business judgment it strives to give the best possible service at the lowest possible cost to the consumer.

> Because of the nature of the business, electric companies like Public Service are regulated monopolies and subject to the supervision of Commissions having legal control over many of their activities. While this is an important factor affecting management and operations, it has not been the driving force behind the success story of the industry... As in other businesses, the workers in all ranks have been and still are and always will be the ones who get things done. Through the exercise of ability, courage, determination and foresight, they have developed one of the most important contributions to our high standard of living....

> Now the light and power business in this country is threatened with a change. For several years many government ownership advocates have been striving to socialize the electric business. Their plan is to create an electric power empire in the hands of the government. . .[T]heir plan strikes at the very heart of our free enterprise system. In the building of electric plants they want to substitute money raised by taxation for private capital and government operation for business management. Their efforts if successful, would tend to destroy initiative and efficiency and to encourage further invasion into other fields of private business.

> Believing with Abraham Lincoln that "In all that the people can individually do so well for themselves, the government ought not to interfere"

we propose to continue our resistance to further socialization of all businesses and the electric light and power industry in particular.

The views expressed by Schiller and other business leaders both in and outside of the utility industries prevailed. Ultimately, interest in public ownership waned. However, for many years those interested in the socialization of the industry continued to fester public opinion against PSNH and other electric firms when the industry began to face the problem of rising fuel costs in the next decade.

Growth for the last half of the 1940s surpassed that in the first half of the decade. Sales as measured in kilowatts and dollars increased by 58 percent. By the twenty-fifth anniversary of PSNH and fiftieth anniversary of combined Manchester Traction-Public Service, the company provided retail services to more than 70 percent of the state's population. In addition, PSNH supplied the majority of the remaining areas with wholesale electricity.

In an address given at the twenty-fifth anniversary dinner of PSNH, Schiller closed his comments with the following thoughts:

> For twenty-five years we have worked together in fair weather and storm, in peace and in war, to bring better service at low cost to people of New Hampshire. We have lighted the streets and roads of your communities. We have lightened the housewife's tasks. We have made less difficult the farmer's toil. We have increased industrial capacity and productivity. Within our lifetime we have watched electricity take its place in the life of the community and play its part in raising the standard of living for this nation to the highest on earth.

> In spite of the fact that our predecessor electric companies were among the first to be found anywhere, we are not now a collection of ancient people or antiquated facilities. We have never hesitated to pioneer. Until it was seized by the Federal Government [for the war effort] in 1945, we owned and operated the first real floating power plant. We now own and operate the only mercury-steam (binary) cycle plant ever built as such from the ground up... We have developed and utilized New Hampshire's water powers intelligently and have coordinated these developments with an adequate system of fuel-burning plants so that neither drought nor flood can threaten seriously the electric supply of the area.

> Our Company, in its first quarter century, has given a good account of itself. We have built well. Our rates compare favorably with any in New

England. No product on the market today has held the line against inflation and increasing costs as well as electricity. The interruptions to service on our lines are few although the climate and weather are not always favorable here in New Hampshire....

We of Public Service Co. of New Hampshire have built up our business without federal grants or subsidies. We have paid taxes fully in proportion to our stature. We have done our best to be good citizens and neighbors. These things we recognize with pride tonight as we look back over the past twenty-five years, but more important than that, we face the future with complete confidence in our ability to carry on and determination to make a history of further success in the future. In this effort may we all be associated for many years to come.

PSNH line crew.

Chapter 10

In Search of Alternative Power Sources

In an unprecedented move in 1950, Public Service Co. of New Hampshire sold one of its local distribution facilities. That retail business, servicing approximately 1100 customers in the Enfield-Canaan area, was isolated from other PSNH territories. The facilities and franchises were sold to Granite State Electric Co. Granite State had a stronghold in the retail business in that part of the state. Prior to this divestiture, PSNH always was the purchaser of franchises.

Public Service Co. of New Hampshire returned to its more familiar role in June 1954, when it acquired the New Hampshire Electric Co.'s capital stock in exchange for a $2.25 million note and 120,000 of its own common stock. For many years the firm would be run as a wholly owned subsidiary corporation rather than being absorbed into the PSNH corporation. New Hampshire Electric Co. was the largest independent electric supplier in the state. Its roots could be traced to the Electric Light Co. of Portsmouth. It serviced thirty-four communities and approximately 20,000 customers in the seacoast area. In addition to providing wholesale electricity to the municipal facility at Rindge, New Hampshire, and the Exeter-Hampton Electric Co., New Hampshire Electric Co. wholesaled across the state border to its own wholly owned subsidiary in Kittery, Maine. The company generated its own electricity from a steam plant in Portsmouth and two hydro-electric plants located in Newmarket and Troy, New Hampshire.

Two years later in 1956, Public Service Co. of New Hampshire purchased the municipal facility in Rindge. Prior to the acquisition

PSNH had been wholesaling electricity to Rindge through its New Hampshire Electric Co. subsidiary. At both the state and national levels private ownership appeared to be winning over state ownership in the utility industry.

On December 31, 1954, Public Service Co. of New Hampshire sold its Manchester bus system to Manchester Transit, Inc., a private company, for $75,000. Manchester Transit, Inc. was a new corporation organized by John Moran and Thomas Burke. They had served as the superintendent and assistant superintendent of the bus line when it was owned by PSNH. The divestiture, as the sale of its gas property in 1946, was in keeping with the company's plan to limit its activities to the electric utility industry. There was little logic to PSNH operating a bus system. It was based on the historic fact of owning the trolleys that preceded the motor coaches. The bus system ran under the new ownership until 1969 when the bus line was sold to Union Street Railway, a holding company with four transit properties. In subsequent years, as a result of increasing costs and declining ridership, the line ran deficits. In 1973, it was acquired by the city for $180,000. The city continues to subsidize its operation under the Manchester Transit Authority.

Public Service Co. of New Hampshire, like other utility companies throughout the country, was searching for alternative power sources to meet the growing demand for its electric output. The consuming public had concern with coal and petroleum as sources of generating electricity due to the impact of increasing costs of these natural resources on electric rates. In 1949, the New Hampshire Public Utilities Commission authorized PSNH to add to its regulated electric rates a "fuel and purchasing power adjustment." As would be expected, the consuming public did not look favorably on the increases it experienced. The company published its rate position in 1951:

> As long as there continues to be so much political significance attached to the subject of electric rates, just so long will they continue to occupy a position in the public eye and the press of the nation which is all out of proportion to their economic significance. To electric utility operators, it is difficult, if not impossible, to understand why the general public seems to accept as inevitable the fact that the costs of all other goods and services... have gone up to meet rising operating costs and at the same time

Lineman repair damage following a storm, about 1945.

seem to think that the electric industry is staffed by supermen... [who] can hold the line... [on] the cost of doing business. Of course, such an attitude on the part of the public is encouraged and abetted by the advocates of government ownership to such a degree that acceptance of it by the public is not only unfair to the electric industry but an aid to those seeking to socialize the industry.

Most of the Company's electric rates are lower than those prevailing before the war... Reductions were made in both 1946 and 1947... As a partial offset to the 1946 and 1947 reductions and as a protection against mounting fuel costs, there was made effective on April 1, 1949, a stop loss feature in the Company's electric rates which minimizes the effect of variations in the cost of fuel on net income. When the cost of fuel is high, the Company collects more money for electricity than when the cost of fuel is low.

The public took issue with the energy sources of the new plants put on line in the 1940s, questioning why they were not hydroelectric plants, which would be immune to inflationary pressure caused by rising fuel prices. In an attempt to explain the company's decision not to build water-generating facilities, PSNH presented the following argument:

The company owns and operates thirty-one hydroelectric plants having an aggregate name-plate rating of 77,500 kilowatts which have an effective capacity of about 38,500 kilowatts in times of low water. Because of the limited availability of water power and to assure an adequate supply of electricity at all times, the Company also owns and operates six fuel-burning plants having an aggregate name-plate rating of 111,750 kilowatts and an effective capability of 122,000 kilowatts.

> Because the water powers are operated at all times to make the most effective use of the water available from time to time, they have been able to produce, during the past few years, 40 to 50 percent of the total annual quantity of electricity. However, in spite of the fact that they were able to produce about 48 per cent of the total annual firm power requirements in 1950, their proportionate ability to assist in carrying the system's peak load was only about 33 per cent during the months of low stream flow... A failure to realize the impact of this inherent characteristic of New Hampshire water power is the major cause of the failure on the part of many people to have a better understanding of water power value.

The document went on to present four reasons why additional hydroelectric power construction could play but a limited goal in meeting future needs:

> In the first place, the topography and geography of the area definitely restrict the possibility of high dams. Second, the rivers vary annually and seasonally through a broad range both as to quantity of water and duration of flow. Third, the ultimate possibilities of most sites usually cannot be realized without serious dislocations of industry, agriculture, and other activities affecting the basic economy of the area. Fourth, the better hydroelectric sites in general already have been developed and, therefore, future hydro developments will have associated with them relatively larger fuel-burning plants if all of the electrical needs of the area are to be supplied all of the time.

Public Service Co. of New Hampshire's words were put into action in 1952, when it completed a second 40,000-kilowatt unit at the Schiller plant, doubling the capacity in the Portsmouth facility. A third unit was added in 1955 to increase the capacity to 120,000 kilowatts. At that point, the plant represented over 40 percent of PSNH's total capacity of 291,000 kilowatts.

In 1954, Public Service Co. of New Hampshire and eleven other New England electric companies formed the Yankee Atomic Energy Co. This alliance was undertaken to share the cost of constructing an atomic power plant in Rowe Township, Massachusetts. The plant, which was to have a capacity of 134,000 kilowatts, was estimated to be completed in 1960. The output of the nuclear plant would be purchased by the participating utilities. By the end of the decade, PSNH had invested $1.4 million in Yankee Atomic Energy Co.

In addition to this experiment in atomic energy, Public Service continued to build conventional steam facilities. In 1957, yet another addition to the Schiller plant increased capacity from 120,000 to 172,000 kilowatts. A new steam plant located in Bow, New Hampshire, with a capacity of 100,000 kilowatts, was scheduled for completion in 1960.

It is useful to summarize the status of Public Service as it entered the 1960s. Its outlook, like that of the country, was tranquil. The fuel and purchase power adjustment, authorized by the Public Utilities Commission in 1949, made swings in energy costs manageable. In addition, mild inflation in other costs at the wholesale level were made tolerable as a result of periodic rate increases allowed by the New Hampshire Public Utilities Commission. In the same way, the cost of living increases in wages throughout the country made the mild inflation at the consumer level tolerable. While there were periodic outcries by the consumers in reference to electric costs, they were mild in comparison to what would follow in the 1960s and 1970s. In the 1950s, the company experienced a 140 percent increase in revenue and net income. This again paralleled the national economy. The company had over 25,000 stockholders, who were satisfied with the firm's profitability and proud of its management.

There was every reason for the country and the firm to look optimistically to the coming decade. No one anticipated the future acceleration in the rate of inflation. Few could imagine how the Vietnam War would divide the country. None could predict how nuclear energy would divide PSNH's customers, investors and the citizens of New Hampshire.

First day on the New York Stock Exchange.

Chapter 11

A New York Stock Exchange Listing

The tranquility within the United States would come to an end in the 1960s, as the result of the assassination of President Kennedy, the expansion of America's participation in the Vietnam Conflict and the accelerating inflation associated with President Johnson's "guns and butter" attempt to finance both the increasing military obligation together with his "Great Society." Public Service Co. of New Hampshire would not experience significant difficulty until the beginning of the following decade. In fact, increased production associated with technological improvements and planned capacity expansions allowed the company to withstand the accelerating inflation of the 1960s.

In its 1961 annual report, the company explained in detail that on July 1 of that year, Yankee Atomic Electric Co. at Rowe, Massachusetts, was place in commercial use. Yankee was the first of four nuclear plants built in New England in which PSNH would participate with a minority ownership share. The company announced:

> Not only was it was completed ahead of schedule, but also at a cost some $13,000,000 less than the original $57,000,000 estimate. Also, it generated its first billion kilowatt-hours in a shorter space of time than ever before accomplished by a nuclear power plant, and produced substantially more than one billion kilowatt-hours from the first charge of atomic fuel put into the reactor. From this favorable combination of circumstances, the plant was able to better original production cost estimates....

> This Company [PSNH] shares the ownership of Yankee with nine other

interconnected New England utilities, which as a group paid $20,000,000 in cash for 20,000 shares of Yankee common stock. This company's proportionate participation was 7 percent or $1,400,000. Because the plant was built at a cost substantially less than originally estimated, the amount of common was reduced pro-rata, among the participants... leaving a net investment of $1,073,800 by this Company in Yankee.

The following year, The Edison Award was presented by The Edison Electric Institute to Yankee Atomic Electric Co. "in recognition of its distinguished contribution during the year 1961 in the development of electric light and power industry for the convenience of the public and the benefit of all." Based on this glowing report it appeared that further joint nuclear plant investments appeared warranted.

Public Service's second involvement was a five percent participation in Connecticut Yankee Atomic Power Co. The plant located in Haddam Neck, Connecticut, was completed in 1968. It had a 560,000-kilowatt capacity powered by the world's largest commercial reactor. Before the end of the decade, PSNH was also participating in the construction of the Maine Yankee Atomic Power Co. plant in Wiscasset, Maine, and the Vermont Yankee Nuclear Power Corp. plant in Vernon, Vermont.

Continuing its campaign against the movement for public ownership of utilities, Schiller had PSNH publish the following statement in its 1962 annual report:

> The Company, far from being a soulless corporation, is the public image of many responsible individuals who recognize certain obligations to those affected by their efforts. In order to meet these obligations, the achievement of each of the following objectives is of utmost importance:
>
> 1. To provide adequate, dependable service at the lowest possible cost.
>
> 2. To provide a reasonable return to investors upon the cash they have invested to build the Company, and to maintain the integrity of the investment.
>
> 3. To provide employees with a fair day's pay for a fair day's work, and to encourage loyalty, self-reliance, and initiative.
>
> 4. To be a good citizen in the fullest sense of the word with complete

recognition of the obligations as well as the privileges which are part of good citizenship.

It is felt that these objectives can best be attained under the traditional American free enterprise system which has made our nation so great among the nations of the world. In spite of this, there are those, both at home and abroad, whose present efforts are directed toward the centralization of control of the nation's entire economy and more particularly toward the nationalization of the investor-owned electric industry. There are those who, for reasons best known to themselves, scorn the free enterprise system as outdated and unworkable in the twentieth century. They think they see salvation in an omnipotent central government in whose service *all* people would labor, thus shackling the dynamic force of individual initiative and reward which have made ours the greatest nation. It is not enough to resent such doctrines personally in silence. We should all make our belief in and dedication to the traditional American way known to those who represent us in government at all levels.

In an effort to meet the first of the four objectives listed above, Public Service Co. of New Hampshire continued to provide increased capacity during the 1960s. In October 1960, the coal-fired 100,000-kilowatt Merrimack Plant in Bow went into operation. The following year this capacity increase was partially offset when the 30,000-kilowatt floating power plant, the *Resistance,* was sold to the Korean Electric Co. However, in 1965 the company announced that an expansion would be made at the Merrimack Plant. The following year ground was broken for Merrimack II which was projected to increase capacity by 250-350,000 kilowatts. In May 1968, Merrimack II went on line.

In addition to expanding its own production capacity and participating as a minority owner in the various Yankee nuclear power projects, PSNH was negotiating with other major New England electric utilities to form a power pool, whereby the companies would exchange excess capacities. Prior sharing had been conducted on an informal basis for over twenty years. In 1967, eleven major electric utilities throughout New England preliminarily approved the New England Power Pool (NEPOOL) to formalize cooperative sharing of power. Power pooling and interconnections between major utilities in a region had the endorsement of the Federal Power Commission.

On May 20, 1968, based on the ever-increasing power needs in the state, the tentative power agreement and the success of the various Yankee power projects, Public Service Co. of New Hampshire announced plans to construct an 860,000-kilowatt nuclear plant in Seabrook, New Hampshire. The project, which had an original estimated cost of $208 million in 1968 dollars, would be built jointly with United Illuminating Co.

An atomic or nuclear power plant is similar to a fossil fuel power plant except that the source of heat used to run the steam driven generators is created by nuclear fission rather than burning coal or gas. While the nuclear energy promised economies in fuel requirements, it created two concerns among environmentalists. The first apprehension involved potential damages from a nuclear accident at the plant and the problems of long-term storage of nuclear waste. The second concern involved the tremendous amount of water that would be needed to cool the steam before it was recycled through the system. Plans called for the water used in the cooling process to be drawn from and returned to the ocean. Environmentalists warned about the impact of the increase in water temperature could be detrimental to plant and animal life in the ocean.

At the time of the announcement, PSNH envisioned participation as co-owners or purchasers of unit power by the various New England power companies that had invested in the other Yankee power companies. There was a general reluctance of other New England power companies to participate in the project. In addition PSNH was faced with the need for a more immediate increase in power capacity than could be anticipated in the nuclear plant project. The following year, Public Service reluctantly elected to defer indefinitely the construction of the Seabrook Nuclear Station. The company took a onetime charge against income for the total costs involved with its preliminary investment. The impact on the net income after taxes amounted to just under $2 million.

In 1965, William Tallman replaced Avery Schiller as president of the company. Schiller remained the chief executive officer of PSNH and assumed the position of chairman of the board. In their joint letter to the stockholders printed in the 1968 annual report the chairman and president issued this prophetic warning:

In the past, the electric utility industry has been able to offset the impact of increasing costs with technological advances and operating efficiencies. However, inflation, if not halted or at least kept within reasonable bounds, can outstrip the most dramatic breakthroughs in technology and improvements in operating efficiency.

The following year's annual report boasted of a decade of growth in service, revenue, operating income and earnings per share. Operating earnings per share had risen from $1.52 in 1959 to $2.36 in 1969. Lest the reader presume that this was at the expense of the rate payer, the 1969 report explained:

> During the decade of the 1960s, inflation has been a way of life. During the period, the Consumers Price Index has increased 25.8%. The prices of almost all conceivable items used in industry, commerce and in the home from heavy machinery to a loaf of bread have succumbed to inflationary pressure. However, the price of electricity has been a notable exception to the general rule. It not only has held the line against inflation but actually has tended downward over the entire ten-year period.

> The record, as far as Public Service Company of New Hampshire is concerned, reflects three general rate reductions. It shows that all electricity sold to ultimate consumers in 1969 was billed at an average price which was 18 percent lower than the average billing price in 1959.

Following the decade of the 1960s, two significant milestones for the company occurred in 1970. On May 14, Avery R. Schiller retired after more than forty-seven years of service to PSNH and its predecessor companies. William C. Tallman became the chief executive officer of Public Service Co. retaining the title of president. Schiller was elected an Honorary Director and named Chairman Emeritus. When Schiller passed away in 1974 The company published the following tribute:

> Avery Schiller's name has been synonymous with the electric utility industry in New Hampshire for many years [After reviewing his career the tribute went on to state:] Numerous honors were bestowed upon Avery during his career, including Fellow, Institute of Electrical and Electronic Engineers; Doctor of Laws, New England College, 1953; University of New Hampshire's Charles Holmes Pettee Medal for "confidence in and devotion to the State of New Hampshire"; Citizen of the Year Award by Manchester Chamber of Commerce, 1958; Engineer of the Year, N.H.

PSNH's headquarters for years was in the New Hampshire Plaza on Elm Street in downtown Manchester.

Society of Professional Engineers, 1966. Many people in the Company and in New Hampshire consider it a privilege to have been called his friend and associate.

The second major milestone reached in 1970 was PSNH's listing on the New York Stock Exchange. Under Schiller, the company had grown to meet all of the financial requirements. The company's decision to seek the prestigious listing was twofold: First, it benefitted existing stockholders by improving the marketability of their stock. Second, the listing would facilitate future public offerings of stocks and bonds, that would be required when the firm reactivated its plan to build the Seabrook nuclear plant.

It is difficult but critical to separate in one's mind Public Service Co. of New Hampshire, the operating company, from PSNH, the firm that built Seabrook and ultimately fell into bankruptcy as a result of this investment. William Frain, Jr., former president of the utility company, regrets that the public's view on PSNH is so clouded by the Seabrook issue that sufficient credit is not given to the basic performance of the utility. Frain, who played a major role during the merger of PSNH into Northern Utilities as a result of the Seabrook induced bankruptcy, supports his view on the service of the firm in stating:

> During the eventual absorption of PSNH into Northeast Utilities, we were determined to adopt the best practices of the two firms. That is, on various issues in operations we examined the procedures at PSNH and at NU. It was decided that whichever practice worked best would be adopted by the other operating company. We at PSNH more than held our own.

Seabrook construction gets under way.

Chapter 12

Seabrook

While the first half of the decade of the 1970s was less than optimum due to regulatory delays in rate increases, there were several positive occurrences. On September 16, 1970, PSNH's stock was accepted for trading on the New York Stock Exchange under the ticker symbol PNH. That same year the company broke ground on a 400,000-kilowatt oil-fired plant in Newington. The plant was completed on schedule four years later. All in all not a bad way to start off a new decade.

In June 1971, PSNH acquired the Greenville Electric Lighting Co. for 15,000 shares of Public Service common stock. The company, in southwestern New Hampshire, was a retail distributor to approximately 1,000 customers. Prior to the acquisition, Greenville purchased its power requirements from PSNH. In July of the following year, PSNH obtained the distribution system of the New Ipswich Light Department. With this purchase, the town of Wolfeboro in the northern part of the state remained the only significant municipal franchise within the territory that PSNH serviced.

In November 1971, the major New England electric companies signed the New England Power Pool Agreement. PSNH cited the advantages in its 1971 annual report:

> The basic objectives of NEPOOL are reliable and maximum economy while maintaining a proper balance between pool electric facilities and the environment....
>
> The development of NEPOOL has made possible to reactivate plans to

construct the Seabrook Nuclear Generating Station which was indefinitely deferred in 1969... Intensive engineering, economic, and environmental studies demonstrate without question that the installation of nuclear generating capacity will result in the production of needed base-load power at the lowest possible cost with the minimum adverse environmental impact consistent with today's technology.

While the New England power companies finally reached an agreement on NEPOOL, PSNH was not as fortunate in reaching an agreement on its July 8, 1971, filing with the Public Utilities Commission of New Hampshire for an increase in its tariffs, or schedule in utility rates for various utility services. This requested increase of 13 percent was the first since 1959. The company defended its position with the following arguments in the 1971 annual report:

> Total electric revenue in 1971 amounted to $80,126,076, an increase of $8,372,000 or 11.7% over 1970. Despite this increase in total electric revenue, earnings per share decreased 12%. This reduction in earnings in the face of substantial growth in revenue is attributable to a rapid across-the-board increase in the cost of doing business. Some of the factors accounting for this rise are increases in the cost of fuel and purchasing power, increased real estate taxes, and higher interest rates....

> Public Service reduced rates three times during the 1960s when inflationary trends spiraled unchecked throughout the general economy... [F]rom December, 1961 until December, 1971, the Consumer Price Index increased 36.9%, while the cost of 250 kilowatt-hours of residential electricity on Public Service lines decreased by 5.4%, from $9.13 to $8.64....

> In light of this enviable record, the approximate 13% increase the Company is seeking certainly appears modest, and not inconsistent with the efforts on the part of the Federal government to combat inflation.

After a considerable delay the Public Utilities Commission acquiesced to approximately half of the 13 percent requested increase. However, at the same time it rescinded the fuel adjustment clause. PSNH went on to appeal the commission's decision.

It is useful for the reader to keep in mind three facts when considering the company's statement in the 1971 annual report. First, the government policy mentioned was the wage and price controls introduced under the Nixon administration in 1971. Second, the 36.9 percent increase over the ten years ending December 31, 1971 rep-

William C. Tallman contemplates the Seabrook issue.

resented an annual compounded rate of 3.2 percent. While these rates were high in comparison to the prior ten years, it was modest relative to total inflation of 128.3 percent or an average annual compounded rate of 8.6 percent during the ten years ending in December 1981. In that next ten-year period, three years would post double-digit inflation. Finally, in 1970 PSNH's interest on new debt reached an all-time high of 9.0 percent. However, since interest rates are both a cause and effect of inflation, this also was mild in comparison to the rates that would follow.

The 1972 annual report published the following update on the proposed nuclear plant:

Seabrook Project, a major nuclear generating station consisting of two 1,150,000 kilowatt units to be owned jointly by the Company (which will own 50% of the project.) and at least eight other utilities in New England, has been proceeding during the past year through the initial planning stages. Some milestones of the year are as follows:

1/20/72 - Board of Directors vote to proceed with project

2/1/72 - Filing of Application with Site Evaluation Committee and Public Utilities Commission

3/1/72 - Selection of Nuclear Service Division of Yankee Atomic Electric Co. - Engineering

3/15/72 - Selection of United Engineers and Constructors of Philadelphia as architect-engineers.

6/7/72 - Selection of Westinghouse Electric Corp. to provide nuclear

99

steam supply and nuclear fuel fabrication for first six regions.

6/19/72 - Start of hearings before Site Evaluation Committee and Public Utilities Commission

12/12/72 - Completion of Company's direct case in siting hearings.

The progress statement in the 1972 annual report ended with the following upbeat comment:

The project is currently on schedule with the first unit to be operational by November 1979, and the second unit by September 1981. The Company's [50%] investment in the project, exclusive of substations and transmission lines, will be approximately $570 million.

In the 1973 annual report, PSNH expressed its regret that the rate increase requested back in July 1971 had yet to be resolved. They reported that 1973 earnings per share had declined an additional 11.9 percent to $2.22 per share despite revenue increasing 14.8% to $108.6 million. The figures from 1970 to 1973 are even more dramatic. Revenue increased 51.3 percent while earnings per share decreased 9.4 percent. While the approval of approximately 50 percent of PSNH's requested increase by the Public Utilities Commission resulted in earnings in 1973 to be above the 1971 level, they fell far short of the inflation adjusted requirement. Obviously, this was bad news for PSNH's shareholders. It also increased the cost of obtaining the funds necessary to finance the company's planned expansion.

The company reported interim status on the rate case as follows:

While some progress has been made in the New Hampshire retail rate case originally filed on July 8, 1971, it has been necessary to continue efforts to obtain adequate rate relief. On December 21, 1973, the New Hampshire Public Utilities Commission issued its Order allowing the Company a 5½ percent increase in the base rate, plus a fuel adjustment clause. The Commission's previous order, which was vacated by the New Hampshire Supreme Court, had allowed a 7 percent increase, but denied a fuel clause.

Your management is grateful that the Commission has acknowledged the necessity of a fuel adjustment charge. Nonetheless, the allowed rates are not adequate... the Company is again seeking redress through an appeal filed with the New Hampshire Supreme Court on February 15, 1974.

In PSNH's mind the requested rate increase, fuel adjustment allowance and the move to nuclear energy all appeared critical in light of accelerating inflation and the Arab oil embargo. In reference to this issue the annual report stated:

> The nation is now faced by the dilemma of an unparalleled energy crisis precipitated by a shortage of oil resulting from the Arabian oil embargo. To meet this crisis, the Company has endeavored to curtail energy consumption and promote conservation at all levels. [However, because of long run growth in demand,] it appears that the best possible solution to the energy crisis is for the nation to shift away from an oil and gas energy economy and to move into a coal-nuclear-electric energy economy as rapidly as possible.

In reference to the Seabrook project, the company reported that the New Hampshire Site Evaluation Committee had approved the Seabrook site for construction and operation of a nuclear plant and the Public Utilities Commission had issued a siting certificate on January 29, 1974.

Subsequent delays in obtaining the necessary Federal approval caused the company to announce a delay in groundbreaking from October, 1974 to July, 1975. This pushed back the estimated completion dates to 1980 and 1982. More important, since inflation was rapid, the estimated cost increased by $60 million.

In non-Seabrook matters, the situation was substantially better. The 400,000-kilowatt Newington Station was activated on June 30, 1974. This plant's capacity was deemed critical until the Seabrook facility became a reality.

Since PSNH's earnings were depressed because of the failure to reconcile the 1971 rate request, the firm's cost of raising over $66 million in new long-term debt and equity in 1974 was higher than it would have been. The 12.75 percent cost of the new debt was a reflection of the firm's downgraded bond rating as a result of depressed earnings and the 1974 inflation rate of 12.5 percent.

On December 31, 1974, the July 1, 1971, rate request was finally resolved. The company summarized the results of the rate agreement:

> The lengthy 3½ year case included three interim Commission decisions
> and two appeals to the New Hampshire Supreme Court... The Commission
> Order released revenues which had been billed under bond during 1972 and
> 1973 amounting to $3.7 million, which had not been reflected in earnings.
> As a result, 1972 and 1973 earnings per share will be restated to $2.62 and
> $2.55, respectively, increases of $0.10 and $0.33, respectively... Earnings
> per share in 1974 were $2.53.

The problems of regulatory delays were not unique to PSNH or
New Hampshire. In his 1988 book, *The Regulation of Public Utilities,*
Charles F. Phillips, Jr., said:

> The environment within which public utilities operate has changed
> dramatically... For some sixty years–up until 1968–the tremendous ex-
> pansion of the entire public utility sector was accomplished in a favorable
> and supportive environment. Economic growth was unquestioned. Annual
> inflation rates, as well as interest rates, were low. Utilities could plan,
> construct, and finance new plants in a relatively short period of time, and
> without great difficulty. Six to eight-year planning periods for new gen-
> erating facilities, for instance, were common. Capacity and reserves were
> adequate. Rates, due to the achievements of economies of scale and sales
> growth, were relatively constant or declining... The regulatory process
> was geared to this environment... For both the regulated and the regulator,
> however, the environment was to change...

> Beginning in the late 1960s, a series of events impacted on the econ-
> omy which altered the environment within which public utilities operated.
> The annual rate of inflation began to accelerate, affecting both operating
> and construction costs. Productivity advances were no longer adequate to
> offset such cost increases. Interest rates started to rise, forcing the cap-
> ital-intensive utilities to pay record-high costs for their new capital. The
> combination or rising costs and high interest rates caused almost immediate
> coverage problems, widespread bond downgrades, and even higher interest
> costs. Fuel prices, for electric and gas utilities, started to escalate.

> Inevitably, utility rates began to rise. Consumers started to organize
> and to intervene in rate cases in opposition of such increases... The me-
> dia, after years of neglect, began to cover utility hearings, often giving
> them top coverage, and to discuss the major issues confronting the entire
> public utility sector... The judicial branch also became more involved in
> the regulatory process... [R]ate cases were often appealed either by the

Protestors at Seabrook construction site.

affected utility or by an intervenor

The year 1975 was the final year in which Public Service Co. of New Hampshire experienced reasonable tranquility. While opponents to nuclear energy spoke out against Seabrook from its conception, the opposition was small and restrained. A national poll conducted by Lewis Harris Associates suggested that only 19 percent opposed building more nuclear plants while 63 percent favored more construction.

Earnings per share rose 11 percent to $2.81. The company increased the annual dividend from $1.64 to $1.80. This first dividend increase in five years did not fully compensate for the inflation over that time period. Nonetheless, it would partially compensate the stock investors and at the same time facilitate the sale of additional stock that would be needed for the Seabrook project.

In July of 1975, the Environmental Protection Agency approved the Seabrook cooling system. The system was designed to use sea water through underground tunnels to cool the plant. In November, following fifty-eight days of hearings before an Atomic Safety and Licensing Board, the Nuclear Regulatory Commission proceedings on PSNH's Seabrook application were brought to a close. At the year's end, the company was optimistic that approval would soon follow.

However, on February 4, 1976, PSNH was informed that hearings would be reopened. In many respects this can be looked upon as the beginning of the end. The following month Seabrook residents voted against construction of the plant, 768 to 632. While this vote ultimately would not hamper the construction, it was indicative of growing concern with nuclear power. On July 7, the NRC approved construction permits, only to cancel them a few days later. The rationale was to allow time for new national standards to be written on nuclear waste disposal.

On July 13, the Clamshell Alliance was formed. This group of anti-nuclear protesters aimed to stop the Seabrook project. On August 1, eighteen protesters were arrested when the group attempted to occupy the Seabrook site. Four days later, a groundbreaking ceremony was conducted following NRC approval. At the ceremony three protesters were arrested. Toward the end of the month 179 persons were arrested in another protest.

The fall and winter demonstrated the waffling by government agencies responsible for overseeing nuclear plant construction. On September 27, the NRC appeals board suspended the Seabrook construction permit. Eight days later the NRC reinstated the permit. On November 8, the Regional EPA Director rejected the plant's cooling system, which caused the NRC appeals board to again pull the permit in January 1977.

In May of that year, 1,414 protesters were arrested, capping off the largest nuclear power protest to date. The attendance record would be broken on June 24,1978, when upwards to 10,000 demonstrators attended a Clamshell demonstration at Seabrook.

Prior to the demonstration on June 17, 1977, the national director of the EPA overruled the regional director's rejection of the cooling system. July brought renewal of the construction permit by the NRC appeals board. As might be expected, this brought on additional court challenges. On February 15, 1978, the Federal appeals court in Boston rejected the evaluation procedure for the cooling system and sent the decision back to the EPA. This led to yet one more suspensions of the permit on June 30 resulting in construction being halted on July

21, 1978. The following month the national EPA reaffirmed its approval, and the NRC reinstated the construction permit on August 11. This in turn ignited a series of eight protests between August 1978 and October 1979 in which a total of 298 individuals were arrested. The last of these eight protests, was the most violent. It lasted from October 6 to the 10. About 2,000 protesters tried unsuccessfully to gain access to the Seabrook construction site. While only twenty-two people were arrested, the state police had to use mace, guard dogs and tear gas to quell the protesters.

In the political arena, Hugh Gallen, Democratic candidate for governor, defeated the incumbent Republican Governor Meldrim Thomson on what many people called a one-issue campaign.

As with most of its sister utility corporations throughout the country, Public Service Co. of New Hampshire's rate base included CWIP (construction work in process) as well as current operating plants. In the 1978 campaign, Republican Governor Thomson spoke in favor of the Seabrook project and supported CWIP as part of the rate base. The Democratic Candidate Gallen professed to be in favor of Seabrook but opposed to rates based on unfinished construction. Following Gallen's election, Zane B. Thurston, Business Editor of the Manchester Union Leader, warned:

> When King Pyrrhus defeated the Romans at Asculum, he soon realized that his victory was gained at too great a cost. Hence, the term "Pyrrhic victory."
>
> New Hampshire consumers, seduced into believing that their electric bill can be miraculously reduced, have gained such a victory...
>
> Governor-elect Gallen, professing to be for Seabrook and against CWIP, is, in effect, claiming to be for motherhood and against pregnancy. Financial experts have testified that Seabrook is impossible without construction work in process–that you can't have one without the other.

Following Gallen taking office in 1979, the New Hampshire Legislature passed an "Anti-CWIP Bill," which the Governor signed into law. The New Hampshire Anti-Construction Work in Process law took effect on May 7, 1979, further hampering PSNH in its attempt to finance the nuclear plant construction.

During this period of time, warding off protests and waging battles in the courts and the State House to keep the construction project moving were not the only problems facing Public Service Co. of New Hampshire. In the hyper inflation of the late 1970s additional delays raised construction and financing costs substantially. Earnings per share in 1979 were $2.56, down 21 percent from the previous year. PSNH was forced to borrow at ever-increasing interest rates. While basic operations of the utility company remained strong, the impact of inflation combined with delays in construction raised both the construction cost and the cost of borrowing. Faced with this increase in costs the company attempted to sell 10 percent of its 50 percent interest in Seabrook. It was successful in only reducing its stake by 3 percent. On December 21, 1979, the Public Utilities Commission granted PSNH an emergency $1.9 million rate hike, which substantially improved operating performance in the following year.

In 1980, Tallman's position was changed from president and chief executive officer to chairman and chief executive officer. R.J. Harrison moved from financial vice president to president.

May 1980 brought its own season of protests. Reporting in the New Hampshire Sunday News, Charles Perkins began his article on the previous day's protest as follows:

> SEABROOK May 24–The Seabrook nuclear power plant, turned into a virtual fortress, held fast today as about 1,400 protestors besieged the construction site with blockades of gates and hit and run assaults on fences. One state trooper was knocked unconscious in a mid-afternoon melee, and other troopers and National Guardsmen became targets for ammonia, bricks and bottles thrown by Coalition for Direct Action members.
>
> An admittedly angry Gov. Hugh J. Gallen told reporters, "They said for the last seven months that this would be a non-violent protest. Now you can see what they mean by non-violent."

The protest continued the next day, but as according to Perkins's report:

> INSIDE SEABROOK STATION–The worst seems over.
>
> Dwindling numbers of Coalition for Direct Action faced increasing aggressive state troopers and National Guardsmen Sunday and failed for a second day to stop construction of the Seabrook nuclear power plant.

By nightfall, several hundred demonstrators remained and assaults on
the perimeter fence were rare.

While the protests were a considerable burden on the state and
PSNH, William Frain, Jr., controller of the firm during those riots and
later president of PSNH commented in 2002, "We could deal with the
protestors. What really hurt was the continual legal challenges."

In 1970, prior to PSNH reactivating its decision to build Seabrook,
it had $142 million in bonds outstanding at an average cost of 5.4
percent. The bonds held an A rating. By the end of 1980 it had $449
million of long-term debt at an average cost of 10.0 percent. Some
of its more recent new debt carried a cost of 17.5 percent. Its rating
had dropped to Baa and Ba. While a large portion of the growth in
debt and the decline in the bond rating could be attributed to the
Seabrook project, the major reason for the increase in the interest rate
was inflation. Even the U.S. Treasury was paying over 14 percent on
its new long-term debt.

Owen "Mac" McQueeney

While the above is useful in evalu-
ating the financial health of PSNH, it is
important to measure the conscience of
the corporation. One way to measure is
to talk with long-term employees. Owen
"Mac" McQueeney, a former employee
of the company, was the third of four
generations to work with PSNH. Mac's
grandfather was a trolley driver for MTL
& P and PSNH. His father was a bus
driver for PSNH. Mac's son works in
energy conservation.

Mac started working for PSNH in 1956 following his graduation
from high school. He advanced from mailroom worker to a lineman
and the moved into management. When he retired in 1994, Mac was
the northern area manager.

Mac made the following observations about PSNH:

I started in the mail room at Public Service. I got to know Mr. Schiller.
He went out of his way to learn people's names. Harrison and Duffett were

similar. They made a point of talking to all of the employees. Working at PSNH seemed like a family. The company created a situation in which you wanted to do the best job that you could do.

Serving the customers was always the most important goal of the company. When power lines went down, workers would always respond to company calls to do the repair work despite the weather conditions.

This dedication did not change when some customers began protesting and criticizing the company for building Seabrook. Providing the best service that we could was always the most important objective.

Some controversy surrounded Seabrook's circulating water system.

Chapter 13

Bankruptcy

W hile opponents of Seabrook were correct in expecting their protests to hamper the Seabrook construction, they did not calculate the reaction of PSNH. The company did not see itself or nuclear energy as the enemy. They spelled out the following in the 1981 annual report:

> Our strategic goals have been carefully designed to accomplish our corporate mission, which is to meet effectively the needs of our customers, employees and shareholders as a financially healthy, investor-owned company which is responsive to the needs of society. The goals are as follows:
>
> To Complete Seabrook Units 1 and 2 as rapidly as possible.
>
> To delay further [non-nuclear] baseload capacity investments as long as possible through efficient utilization of present capacity, aggressive load management, conservation and a vigorous pursuit of available supplemental or minimal investment capacity and energy sources...

The annual report for the following year detailed the progress of the Seabrook construction. The second goal, to add energy sources at minimal investment, was discussed in negotiations to receive surplus power from Canada's Hydro-Quebec and the conversion of the Schiller Station from oil to coal.

Throughout the first half of the 1980s PSNH continued to be a profitable operating company. Earnings per share ranged from $2.65 to $3.49. However, construction and financing costs associated with the Seabrook Project were capitalized, and thus did not have an impact on the earnings. In 1984, the escalating costs associated with Seabrook resulted in the banks becoming increasingly concerned about PSNH's ability to complete the project. They responded by freezing Public Service's line of credit. The company discontinued the $2.12 annual dividend and halted construction at Seabrook for two months. The decision was made to discontinue construction of Unit II. This write-off together with write-offs associated with some of the construction costs associated with Unit I caused PSNH to show negative earnings per share of $6.44 in 1986 and $14.16 in 1987. These bottom-line losses were despite profitable operating income.

By July 1986, Unit I was completed. Unfortunately for PSNH, the meltdown at Chernobyl brought a new round of concerns about the safety of any nuclear plant. The Commonwealth of Massachusetts refused to cooperate with the completion of an emergency evacuation plan. Since the Seabrook plant was within ten miles of the Massachusetts state line, the refusal by the Commonwealth succeeded in further delaying the process. It was not until four years later in August 1990 that Seabrook went on line at full power.

On January 26, 1988, the New Hampshire Supreme Court ruled on PSNH's appeal to suspend the Anti-CWIP legislation. The court upheld the Anti-CWIP legislation. Two days later, PSNH filed for bankruptcy protection under Chapter 11 of the U.S. Bankruptcy Code.

Under the Federal Bankruptcy Code, Public Service Co. of New Hampshire had the option of continuing under the regulation of the New Hampshire Public Utilities Commission or to reorganize under the Federal Energy Regulatory Commission. Because of the difficulty to establish basic rates, the Anti-CWIP legislation and the potential inability to recover costs associated with the Seabrook construction if the plant were never to be licensed, PSNH decided to seek reorganization under FERC jurisdiction. On September 23,1989, U.S. Bankruptcy Judge James Yacos declared that PSNH could seek reorganization outside the jurisdiction of the NHPUC stating, "Like it or not, Congress has decreed that local rule can be determined indirectly by FERC." N.H. Governor Judd Gregg, fearing the worst, was determined to litigate the ruling which he believed would "savage New Hampshire customers for the benefit of out-of-state creditors." With this in mind, the Office of the Governor played an active role in the bankruptcy negotiation process.

The bankruptcy was taking its toll on the employees. In September 15, 1988, PSNH's Harrison resigned for health reasons. He was replaced by John C. Duffett. Duffett held the position of executive vice president and chief operating officer, prior to his promotion to president.

From the date of filing on January 28, 1988, until March 15, 1989, U.S. Bankruptcy Judge James Yacos had granted PSNH an extended period of time in which it had the exclusive right to work

out a reorganization plan. On that date, the Judge ruled other parties could present reorganization plans. Remember that PSNH always was and continued to be a sound operating utility. What was uncertain was the value of Seabrook. During the period of exclusivity, three major New England power groups, New England Electric System, based in Massachusetts, Northeast Utilities, based in Connecticut, and a collaborated effort by Central Maine Power and Central Vermont Public Service Co., indicated interest.

Judge James Yacos

Ultimately Northeast Utilities' proposal was selected. On July 27, 1989, New Hampshire Governor Judd Gregg endorsed NU's plan, which required a series of future fixed-rate increases to ensure that Northeast Utilities would receive a fair return on its purchase of PSNH. On October 25, PSNH owners supported NU's plan which had been increased to $2.3 billion. On November 18, the major creditors accepted the plan. On December 14, the plan was endorsed by the New Hampshire legislature. Since the governor did not have the authority to bind the state without legislative approval, the endorsement was critical for the process to continue. Four days later on December 18, 1989, Governor Judd Gregg signed the bill, which would eventually return rate-setting authority to the NHPUC, into law. U.S. Bankruptcy Judge Yacos determined that the plan was fair and workable.

The New Hampshire State House of Representatives of 1989.

The plan called for seven annual 5.5 percent rate increases. The first took place just two weeks after Governor Gregg signed the bill into law. The second occurred on May 16, 1991, the day PSNH emerged from bankruptcy. The next five went into effect on June 1 of years 1992 through 1996. It was assumed that there would be no further increases for the years 1997, 1998 and 1999. Because of fuel cost savings and other economy measures, the net result for the customers was better then projected. During the seven years of rate increases, the actual costs averaged two percent below schedule. In the three years in which no further increases were planned, the actual costs averaged six percent below schedule. Over the ten-year period, the average savings was three percent.

As well as examining the cost of the reorganization to the rate payer, it is important to consider the impact of PSNH's bankruptcy on its investors. In addition to the common stock, there were several different preferred stock and bond issues. For convenience's sake, the securities can be classified according to the priority of their claims into four groups, mortgage or secured bonds, debenture or unsecured bonds, preferred stock and common stock. Since the mortgage bonds had legal claim to the physical property, they were paid all accumulated interest and principal in cash. The debenture bond holders, who did not have specific claim to particular assets, also received all accumulated interest and principal. However, only 57 percent was in cash. The remaining 43 percent was in new common stock, which was subsequently redeemed by Northeast Utilities for cash.

The preferred stockholders received 95 percent of the par value of their stock, and were not compensated for scheduled dividends that were not paid. Approximately 51 percent was in new common stock that was redeemed by NU and the remaining 44 percent was in promissory notes.

The common stockholders, who always are at the end of the line in the case of bankruptcies, received 27.5 percent of their par value. About 12.8 percent was in new common stock that was subsequently retired by NU. The remaining 14.7 percent was in a promissory note. The 27.5 percent of par value greatly overstates the residual value that the common stockholders received. As late as 1980, the stock sold at $20 a share or four times the $5 par value. If one uses this as the yardstick, the common stockholders, in addition to missing dividends from 1984 on, received only 6.9 percent of their original investment.

Anti-nuclear protestors at the Seabrook gate.

Chapter 14

An Electrifying Controversy

Rhetoric associated with the pros and cons of nuclear power became highly charged. Each side had its own C WORD. Protesters suggested that nuclear plants could cause CANCER. On July 30, 1973, the Massachusetts border town's newspaper, the Newburyport Daily News, reported:

> Peter Randall doesn't want to scare people, but if it's necessary to stop the proposed $1 billion nuclear power plant at Seabrook, he'll do it.
>
> "We've made a point of not trying to put forth scare tactics" said Peter Randall, president of the Seacoast Anti-Pollution League (SAPL).
>
> But things have changed... Construction is proposed to begin in 1975 with partial operation under way four years later.
>
> "New Hampshire has one of the highest *CANCER* rates in the country," Randall said, "and the seacoast has one of the highest in the state. I'm not saying if they build a nuclear plant, everyone would die of *CANCER* around here. But, we don't want that plant down here."

A March 23, 1977, editorial in the New Hampshire Manchester Union Leader, titled "Knaves and Fools," suggests that PSNH President Tallman may have crossed the line in the use of his own C WORD, suggesting that the protest could be a result of COMMUNISM. In part, the editorial said:

> It is inevitable that there will be a spirited and highly emotional reaction to Public Service Company of New Hampshire President William Tallman's statement to the Exeter Rotary Club that much of the opposition to nuclear power stems not only from ignorance, fear and superstition, but

also from *COMMUNIST* "subversion."

Of course, Tallman made it clear that he was not accusing opponents of the proposed Seabrook Nuclear Power Plant of being *COMMUNISTS*. Moreover, he emphasized that he had "no knowledge" of any *COMMUNIST* working influence against the nuclear facility. However, recalling how the Communist East Germans have contributed to unrest in West Germany over nuclear power, he said he "wouldn't be surprised" if the *COMMUNISTS* were "in the background' and that at the very least, most of those who are against nuclear power are people "who don't like the system."

It is beyond the scope of this chapter to review every statement made in favor or opposed to the Seabrook plant. Both sides argued passionately, if not always rationally, for their cause. It also is beyond the scope of this book to present all of the arguments for and against nuclear power. However, it is useful to evaluate the economic and political aspects of the decision by PSNH to invest in Seabrook. In the prior chapter, PSNH's rationale has been presented on a year-by-year basis as various outcomes emerged. Now it is appropriate to review one of the major postmortem criticisms of the utility company and then to present PSNH's own postmortem evaluation.

In the July, 1990 edition of New England Monthly, Edward O. Wells published an article titled "Sunk Costs," in which he severely criticized Public Service Co. of New Hampshire for its actions relative to Seabrook. The author left no uncertainty in the mind of the reader as to his own views. Under the title was the subheading, "How a little New Hampshire utility parlayed an $850 million nuclear reactor into a $6.5 billion fiasco." Wells criticized PSNH in five areas: the location of the plant, the size of the project relative to the size of PSNH, the company's attempt to use CWIP in its rate base, the subsequent method of financing and the decision to continue with the construction against increasing resistance.

In reference to the first of these five topics, Wells wrote:

Various groups objected to the plant on environmental grounds. The plans called for a cooling system that would use 1.2 billion gallons of seawater per day and return that water to a marine estuary thirty-nine degrees warmer. Groups such as the Clamshell Alliance also argued that the plant was inherently dangerous and that the chosen site represented a distinct menace to public safety. Back in 1967, Public Service's own engineering consultant had ranked Seabrook as the least desirable of five possible New Hampshire sites. The nuclear station would, for instance, be situated within a few miles of Hampton Beach, where as many as seventy thousand people bathe on hot summer days, and where narrow access roads provide the only–and clearly inadequate–means of evacuation in case of an accident.

On the size, Wells cited this fact:

> Other utilities taking on ambitious nuclear projects were typically four or five times larger than PSNH. Public Service's relative smallness raised its cost of borrowing money and undermined its creditworthiness.

Wells' view on the inclusion of CWIP in the rate base are cited below:

> Public Service decided to charge its customers for money already spent on Seabrook's construction. In 1978 PSNH, with support from Governor Thomson, had prevailed upon the New Hampshire Public Utilities Commission to allow it to earn a return on $100 million worth of Seabrook-related construction costs.

> This unpopular plan had become the crucial issue in the 1978 gubernatorial campaign, when Democrat Hugh Gallen ran against Thomson. Just weeks before the election, Public Service raised executive salaries and the shareholder dividend. Thomson, the consummate politician and Public Service loyalist, was stunned by the company's politically inept move. "In the last campaign I was fighting their battle," Thomson recalls. "But they had no sense of give-and-take. They were just going to do things regardless. What a bunch of dummies."

Thomson had lost to Gallen in November 1978. The following May, Gallen signed legislation barring Public Service from charging its customers for Seabrook's sunk cost until the plant was completed and generating power.

In reference to the subsequent method of financing, Wells commented on PSNH's use of junk or high-risk bonds:

> Traditionally, utilities have been conservatively managed and financed... Merrill Lynch had created a novel concept: the financing of a utility [PSNH in 1984] with junk bonds. Drexel Burnham Lambert, which dominated the junk bond market, was caught off guard...

Eager to get in on this new action, Drexel arranged a meeting with Public Service in September... with Michael Milken, the notorious master of junk bond financing...

Milken's acumen and facility with numbers impressed [PSNH's President] Harrison. He remembers the performance as "brilliant, fascinating." In the meeting, Milken presented his central "probabilistic theory," which lay behind the whole junk bond phenomenon. It went as follows: If an investor bought a junk bond portfolio of one hundred high-risk issues, five of those would be worthless because the companies would go bankrupt. But that didn't matter; the investor would still be ahead of the game because of the above-average interest paid out by the other ninety-five issues. Harrison was greatly taken with this theory. He seems to have been oblivious to the possibility that his company, PSNH, might fall among the doomed five percent, to the fact that Milken didn't care who were the winners and who were the losers in his portfolios of junk.

PSNH's unwillingness to back away from the Seabrook project, reminded Wells of a conversation of Mike Love, whom Governor Gallen had appointed to head the three-member Public Utilities Commission:

Love says, "Our position at the PUC was, 'If we are going to give you reasonable and timely rate relief, will you please try to realize what you are doing?'" His plea, he claims, went unheeded. "It was like trying to talk to an addict." Love remembers an exchange he had with a Public Service attorney during a financing hearing. "I recall asking him, 'What if the prime rate goes to twenty percent? Would that change the way you

raise money?'

"'No.'

"'Thirty percent?'

"'No.'

"'At what rate do you stop borrowing, or slow down?'

"Their attorney then said there was no rate. There was no limit. They would just keep borrowing until people stopped loaning them money."

In the concluding page of his article, Wells noted:

In the final accounting for Seabrook, one figure stands out. About half of the plant's total cost, more than $3 billion, was spent paying *interest* on borrowed money. Seabrook was built through an orgy of high-cost borrowing...

According to one theory, Public Service's management launched the Seabrook project partly because they feared being taken over; in the end they achieved the opposite result.

After commenting on how many of the key players in the Seabrook project ended up financially well off, Wells concluded:

The people who have paid most dearly for Seabrook are Public Service's long-term stockholders. Utility stock, generally considered a safe investment, attracts the proverbial widows, orphans and retirees of the investment game. In the early 1970s, PSNH stock traded as high as $30.50. Today it is worth only one tenth that and since February 1984 has paid no dividends....

The cost of Seabrook will also fall heavily on households and businesses in New Hampshire....

One can allow that Public Service executives didn't intend to preside over a debacle, and that the financiers only did what was asked of them. But Public Service's managers avowed publicly they would borrow at any cost to get Seabrook built. It seems unlikely that rational people would have pursued such a reckless, uneconomic course if they hadn't known they could always move on and let others pay for the mess they left behind—all $6.5 billion of it.

It is difficult to read the Wells' critique, without reflecting on the quote by Arthur Stone Dewing found in Chapter 7. If one accepts Wells's views, only minor changes, *presented in italics,* need be incorporated to describe PSNH's management. Dewing wrote:

> Four main motives have led men to expand *or alter* business enterprises. On the whole they are not economical, but rather psychological... The most powerful motive that leads a man to expand a business is the illusion of valuing himself in terms of his setting. The bigger the business, the bigger the man... The second motive, less significant... is the creative impulse... [Somewhere] in the mental structure of all of us lies the impulse to build, to see our ideas form in material results... The third motive is the economic... [T]he vast majority of businessmen *in regulated industries* who plan enlargements, consolidations, and expansions of their business are not actuated primarily by the impulse to make more money *or to lower customer's rates*, although they unquestionably place this motive uppermost when they need to present plans for enlargements to directors, stockholders, *regulators or ratepayers.* The fourth motive is the satisfaction in taking speculative chances. . . A successful business manager is invariably a man of imagination. Invariably the man of imagination revels in uncertainties... All men enjoy the game they think they can play.

On the other hand, supporters of PSNH could easily further adjust the quote to reflect their view of those who fought against the Seabrook Nuclear Plant. One could argue that much of the escalation in costs was a result of the anti-Seabrook movement, to wit:

> Four main motives have led *crusaders to challenge* business enterprises. On the whole they are not *environmental or safety motivated,* but rather psychological... The most powerful motive that leads a man to *challenge* a business is the illusion of valuing himself in terms of his setting. *In a David and Goliath view,* [T]he bigger the business *brought down,* [t]he bigger the *crusader*... The second motive, less significant... is the *destructive* impulse... [Somewhere] in the mental structure of all of us lies the impulse to *destroy*... The third motive is the *environment, safety or economy...* [T]he vast majority of *crusaders against businesses* are not actuated primarily by the impulse to *save the environment, protect the public or lower customer's rates*, although they unquestionably place these motives uppermost when they need to present plans to *politicians, regulators or ratepayers.* The fourth motive is the satisfaction in taking speculative chances... A successful *crusader* is invariably a man of imagination. Invariably the man of imagination revels in uncertainties... All men enjoy the game they think they can play.

Economics Professor John Romps of Saint Anselm College made the following observations on Wells' thesis and the ultimate bankruptcy resolution:

> Public Service's construction of the Seabrook Nuclear Power Plant was hurt by five factors that were completely unanticipated when the plans were made in 1972. First, over the next decade inflation would average 9 percent a year. Mr. Wells constantly addresses cost increasing and high interest rates, yet he never mentions the impact of inflation on the construction costs and the cost of financing. He quotes Commissioner Love as asking what would happen if the prime rate reached 20 percent. When the rate did reach that level in early 1981, the real rate, adjusted for inflation, was virtually zero. Given the unexpected inflation and the resulting high interest rates it is not surprising that the cost of the project rose accordingly.

> Second, there was the Oil Embargo and subsequent five fold increase in the price of oil between 1973 and 1980. Wells states, "between 1972 and 1976 the PUC had allowed Public Service's electric rates to rise by 112 percent." In fact there was only one 13 percent regulated rate increase, the only increase since 1959. The rest was the fuel adjustment charge as a result of the 200 percent increase in oil over that time period. It seems problematic to blame Seabrook or PSNH management for the rate hikes. While the oil price increases should have been an argument in favor of Seabrook, in fact their presence hurt Public Service since they impacted on the profitability of the firm. This made it more difficult to attract investors and increased the financing costs.

> Third, the Anti-CWIP Law was passed by the legislature in 1979. Wells implies that CWIP charges were controversial and unusual. In fact, the costs of construction of new plants are routinely included in pricing decisions by regulated utilities as well as unregulated private companies. To suggest that the cost of building the plants was not going to be paid for by ratepayers is absurd. All the Anti-CWIP Law did was to delay the day of reckoning for the public, while increasing the costs astronomically during this period of inflation and high interest rates. In addition this unforeseen reduction in revenue caused a further decline in the company's bond rating thus further increasing the interest rate that had to be paid in order to borrow the money the Anti-CWIP Law required. The cost of Seabrook had to be paid sooner or later. The Anti-CWIP Law assured that it would be later and much higher.

> Fourth, there were the Three Mile Accident and the Chernobyl Di-

saster. Both further increased the fear of the public, causing regulatory delays. PSNH could not have anticipated either event or the degree of public reaction.

Finally, when the plant was completed in July 1986, Massachusetts refused to participation in the evacuation plan that was necessary for the plant to begin operations. The resulting four year delay did nothing to help the company out of the abyss of debt. In fact it contributed to paying interest on interest since PSNH could not include the costs of construction in its rate base until the plant went on line.

While limiting most of his remarks to a critique of Wells's criticism of PSNH, Romps made the following observation as to bankruptcy reorganization under Judge Yacos:

Wells states Drexel Lambert's strategy as espoused by Michael Milken was that junk bond holders anticipated losing on some of their investments because of the risky nature, but the high interest received on the successful investments would more than compensate for the losses. However, despite the high risks associated with the later bond issues, the bankruptcy court saw to it that all bondholders, even those who bought the bonds as junk, knowing the risk, were paid in full. All this did was increase the cost to Northern Utilities requiring even higher future electric bills for the citizens of New Hampshire.

Following the resolution of the bankruptcy, PSNH published a pamphlet titled *New Hampshire's Energy Partnership* in which it chronicled the firm's bankruptcy and reorganization. The approach used was to state facts, without casting blame on others or presenting excuses for the outcome. Portions of the first section captioned "Seabrook Station–A Well-Intentioned Investment," which deal with the rationale behind PSNH's original decision to build and subsequent decisions to continue with the project, are presented here:

Like many electric utilities in the early 1970s, Public Service of New Hampshire (PSNH) believed that investing in a nuclear power plant would be a way to ensure an ample, low-cost energy supply for the future. Nuclear energy was a proven technology in other parts of the United States and the world. PSNH, however, underestimated the public opposition, exhaustive regulatory approvals and historic nuclear-related world events that led to the resulting cost overruns in building and financing Seabrook Station. It is clear that PSNH never expected that this once well-intentioned decision would jeopardize the company's viability and lead to its financial demise....

PSNH encountered little public opposition to Seabrook in the first few years following the company's announcement to build the plant. As PSNH collected needed approvals and construction appeared imminent, vocal opposition developed.

In 1976, the year that Seabrook was awarded a construction permit, the first protest occurred at the planned site. This marked the beginning of more than a decade of protests that were heard both outside the plant and inside regulatory chambers and courtrooms in New Hampshire and Washington.

Public opposition initially centered on the environmental effects of cooling tunnels that would release heated water into the Atlantic Ocean. Following the accident in 1979 at the Three Mile Island nuclear power plant near Harrisburg, PA, protesters began to address public safety issues and the ability to evacuate residents living within 10 miles of the plant... Public outcry over safety issues intensified after the fire and radiation release at Chernobyl in the former Soviet Union in 1986. These protests played a significant role in delaying emergency evacuation plans... further impeding the plan's approval.

In addition to delays imposed through public intervention, slow regulatory approval and two significant labor strikes hampered PSNH. With each delay, Seabrook's cost escalated.

In 1978, PSNH received approval to begin charging customers for the carrying costs on the money it was borrowing to build Seabrook Station, a practice that was widely used by other utilities when constructing major generating facilities... In 1979, [newly elected Governor Hugh Gallen signed] an Anti-CWIP law that prohibited PSNH from charging customers for the cost associated with building Seabrook until the plant was providing electricity to customers. Given the amount of money already invested in Seabrook, PSNH chose to move ahead with the project, despite the financial strains that the Anti-CWIP law would present. The company planned to borrow what it needed to pay for both direct construction costs and interest on loans.

Unitil Service Corp.'s Todd M. Bohan, Ph.D., a former economist with the NHPUC, makes the following observation on the impact of the Anti-CWIP Law:

In thinking about the process PSNH went through leading to the eventual construction and completion of Seabrook Station, it makes one wonder if the Anti-CWIP Law was never passed, would Seabrook ultimately have been completed? If PSNH had been allowed recovery of CWIP (that is, had the Anti-CWIP Low not passed), it then makes one speculate that as the construction costs of Seabrook started to escalate would PSNH have decided to disband the construction, recover its costs it had experienced to date and not push for completion of Seabrook Station?

What hindsight does offer us though is that after-the-fact PSNH faced essentially two options: (1) no recovery of its investment associated with Seabrook Station if it decided to *not* complete construction, or (2) recovery of its investment, subject to regulatory review, if Seabrook Station becomes operational. (In the regulatory jargon this is known as *used and useful*.) Given these two options it becomes understandable why seemingly irrational behavior took over as PSNH, in order to receive recovery of its investment in Seabrook Station, pushed for the financing necessary to complete Seabrook and make it operational. Traditional economic cost/benefit analysis was set aside in favor of borrowing and spending more money in order to recoup money already spent.

In retrospect, both sides experienced victory and defeat. The opponents of Seabrook can claim victory in as much as the second reactor was never built and that the Seabrook plant was both a safer and more environmentally friendly facility. More important, from their perspective, no nuclear plant has been built since Seabrook. The utility industry was put on notice that future construction would include inflated costs associated with legal challenges. On the other hand, the opponents of Seabrook must assume responsibility for a major portion of the escalated rates that New Hampshire customers have paid since Seabrook went on line.

While Public Service's management must assume much of the responsibility for the bankruptcy, they can look with pride on the performance and safety record at Seabrook. Had the legal process allowed Seabrook to be built in a timely manner, not only would it have been an engineering-efficient plant but also a cost-efficient plant.

Chapter 15

Life Under Restructuring

When Public Service emerged from bankruptcy on May 16, 1991, the common stockholders were the former unsecured bondholders, preferred stockholders and old common stockholders who received shares of new common stock as a result of the bankruptcy agreement. At that time, a temporary board of directors was formed. J.P. Tyrell, a retired executive vice president and chief financial officer of Boston Edison, was elected Chairman. L.E. Maglathin, Jr., a former Northeast Utilities' senior officer, was appointed president and chief executive officer. The positions were of an interim nature until Northeast Utilities' acquisition of PSNH could be finalized.

One year later, on June 5, 1992, Northeast Utilities purchased all of the new common stock for $20 each. PSNH's 35.6 percent ownership in Seabrook was transferred to North Atlantic Energy Corp., a Northeast Utilities' subsidiary. At this point, a Northeast Utilities board was elected to the board of directors of PSNH. W.B. Ellis, chairman and chief executive officer of Northeast Utilities became chairman and chief executive officer of its PSNH subsidiary corporation. F.R. Locke, also an Northeast Utilities executive, was appointed president of PSNH.

As might be expected, employment cutbacks would ultimately follow. In 1989, when NU expressed an interest in acquiring PSNH, Ellis announced a plan that would be include no terminations–other than for "just cause"–for an eighteen-month period. Following the eighteen-month period, any employee who was terminated for other then "just cause" would receive 1 to 1½ weeks salary for each six months of employment with the company. In addition minimum severance pay varied from four weeks to nine months, depending on the employee grade level. According to this formula, an employee, with thirty years service, at the middle or lower grade levels, would receive severance pay equal to a salary of sixty weeks. By December 31, 1992, employment totalled 1,640. This was down from the December 31, 1990, high of 2,760. However, almost all of this reduction can be attributed to the Seabrook workers who were no longer counted in the PSNH subsidiary.

Following NU's purchase of the new common stock from the previous bond and stockholders, PSNH's position was similar to its origin some sixty-five years earlier. It was a subsidiary of a holding company. When PSNH began its corporate existence in 1926, as a subsidiary of New England Public Service Co., the first president of PSNH was Walter S. Wyman, an officer of the immediate holding company. Eventually the position was taken over by Avery Schiller. In a similar manner, when PSNH became a subsidiary of Northeast Utilities, the presidency was filled by R. Frank Locke, an officer of the parent company.

Employees noted a distinct decline in company morale following the bankruptcy. In addition to the normal apprehension associated with employment cutbacks were the uncertainties associated with the introduction of outside management and the potential for the subordination of PSNH's mission to Northeast Utilities' overall goals.

However, in a relatively brief period of time, the presidency at PSNH was filled by long-term Public Service employees, first by William Frain, Jr., and in 2000 by Gary Long. Frain described his original employment with PSNH::

> When I graduated from Saint Anselm College [in Manchester, New Hampshire] in 1964, I was determined to stay in New Hampshire. At the same time, I wanted to work for a large company. I went between the telephone company and PSNH seeking employment. Apparently my employment at Public Service was a result of my hounding. I was the first non-engineering college graduate hired by the company in many years. At one point, during the employment process, they told me, "We are im-

pressed with your persistence. We don't know where we will place you, but we decided to hire you."

Frain began in the accounting department, rose to the position of assistant controller in 1971 and then controller in 1979. In 1982, he was appointed vice-president with responsibility for accounting and treasury. He became vice-president with responsibility for customer service and marketing in 1987. On February 1, 1994, William Frain, Jr., a thirty-year PSNH veteran, was the first local employee to assume the role of president and chief operating officer of PSNH under Northeast Utilities. In March, 2000, Frain was appointed chief executive officer of PSNH.

Bill Frain

In addition to overseeing the normal operations of the utility company, Frain's tenure involved three major challenges. First, he wanted to restore the reputation of Public Service Co. of New Hampshire as being a true public servant of the state. His second major challenge involved improving company morale. Finally he had to deal with the movement towards deregulating New Hampshire's electric utility industry.

Frain's involvement with the community exemplified the creed professed by Samuel Insull and Avery Schiller. He was active in the Business and Industry Association of New Hampshire, the Greater Manchester Chamber of Commerce, the New Hampshire Business Committee for the Arts, Saint Anselm College, Junior Achievement, the United Way, the New Hampshire Humanities Council, the Easter Seal Society of New Hampshire and others. He was recognized as Citizen of the Year for 1997 by the greater Manchester Chamber of Commerce in. In 2000, he was named New Hampshire Business Leader of the Decade.

Under Frain's leadership, PSNH and its employees became actively engaged in a wide range of organizations and activities throughout New Hampshire. Over this period PSNH created partnerships and alliances and its significant efforts were recognized by numerous civic, nonprofit, environmental and business organizations. In 1997 PSNH was named Business of the Year in New Hampshire.

The movement in New Hampshire toward deregulating electric utilities was part of a national trend. A July 1997 Wall Street Journal article listed eight states, including New Hampshire, as having passed deregulation laws. The article listed an additional 22 states that had proposed deregulation laws.

Before embarking on a study of the particulars involved with restructuring in New Hampshire, it is useful to review the traditional concept of public utilities. Todd Bohan, a former economist with the New Hampshire Public Utilities Commission, makes the following observations:

> The concept of a *public utility* generally includes an explanation that the service being provided is that of a natural monopoly best provided by one firm in a given geographical area. In addition the service is essential to the public. The rights and obligations of public utilities have evolved over time. There are a number of obligations of a public utility including: serving all customers that are willing and able to pay for the service, providing safe and adequate service, and charging nondiscriminatory and just and reasonable rates to its customers. In return, a *public utility* operates with certain rights including charging reasonable rates for its services and operating with an exclusive right to serve a geographic territory with protection from competition for its services.
>
> The utility paradigm of recent times, prior to Restructuring, is that utilities operate under *exclusive franchise rights*. This suggests that utilities operating under an exclusive service right for the franchise territory have the obligation to serve all, and the privilege of being the only one allowed to serve those in the franchise territory. This exclusivity of utility franchises in New Hampshire would change with a subsequent ruling of the NHPUC.

The New Hampshire deregulation movement can be traced to August 1994, when Freedom Electric Power Co. filed a petition with the NHPUC, requesting permission to compete with PSNH's retail customers. Since Freedom did not have an electric distribution system in PSNH's territory, the request required the distribution be done by PSNH. The following January the NHPUC initiated a series of roundtable sessions to consider electric utility competition. In June 1995, the commission ruled on FEPC's request stating that franchises in New Hampshire are not exclusive as a matter of law. As might be expected, PSNH appealed the ruling to the New Hampshire Supreme Court. The following May, the court upheld the commission's ruling.

In June 1996, the month following the New Hampshire Supreme Court decision, a pilot program began in which competition in the generation of electricity was to be tested. The transmission and distribution of electricity would continue to be regulated. For PSNH and electric utilities in general, electric generation represented about one third of the typical electric bill. Approximately 17,000 customers were eligible to participate. To encourage participation, customers were offered a 10 percent incentive credit from their local utility. A total of thirty-four power suppliers registered to sell energy to the participants.

In addition to addressing the question of retail competition, the 1995 roundtable sessions considered deregulation in general. When the roundtable submitted its report in September 1995, it noted that while the objective was to lower prices for electricity in the long run, restructuring should not be driven by a desire to address immediate concerns about PSNH's rates.

In March 1996, the New Hampshire Legislature passed the Electric Utility Restructuring Act (HB 1392). The act created Chapter 374-F in the New Hampshire Statutes. The primary rationale included in the new statute reads:

> The most compelling reason to restructure the New Hampshire electric utility industry is to reduce costs for all consumers of electricity by harnessing the power of competitive markets. The overall public policy goal of restructuring is to develop a more efficient industry structure and regulatory framework that results in a more productive economy by reducing costs to consumers while maintaining safe and reliable electric service with minimum adverse impacts on the environment. Increased customer choice and the development of competitive markets for wholesale and retail electric services are key elements in a restructured industry that will require unbundling of prices and services and at least functional separation of centralized generation services from transmission and distribution services.

To some observers, this act was an attempt to unilaterally rene-
gotiate the agreement reached between the State and PSNH at the time
of bankruptcy. Specifically, the seven annual 5.5 percent increases
were originally expected to be approximately 1.0 percent a year above
estimated inflation of 4.5 percent. Since inflation in the first half of
the 1990s averaged 3.5 percent the real, i.e. inflation adjusted, rate
was 2.0 percent a year.

While the statute does not mention this as a goal, in the public
law encompassing the restructuring statute, the legislature expressly
stated (emphasis added):

> New Hampshire has the highest average electric rates in the nation and
> such rates are unreasonably high. The general court also finds that *electric
> rates for most citizens may further increase during the remaining years of
> the Public Service Company of New Hampshire rate agreement* and that
> there is a wide rate disparity in electric rates both within New Hampshire
> and as compared to the region.

In April 1996, the month following the passage of the Electric
Utility Restructuring Act, and the month prior to the N.H. Supreme
Court Decision on the exclusive franchises, PSNH proposed its own
plan titled *Customers First*. The program offered a reduction in rates
by 10 percent, consisting of forgoing the final 5.5 percent increase
scheduled for June 1 and to decrease rates further by as much as 4.5
percent. In exchange for the voluntary reduction in rates PSNH called
for a collaboration process of utility companies, state officials, and
representatives of consumers, business and environmental organizations.

In anticipation of the question, "Isn't this proposal a case of too
little, too late?" the company responded:

> *Customers First* is the only proposal that offers near-term savings to
> all PSNH customers. A 10 percent reduction in rates translates into $80
> million in annual savings for customers, or $320 million over four years.
> Also, capping rates at the lower levels through 2000 provides additional
> value and stability for our customers. Others have talked about lower rates.
> This proposal can achieve lower rates.
>
> The state has just begun the utility restructuring process, not just
> ended it. Passage of restructuring legislation is excellent timing for the

introduction of collaboration and the *Customers First* proposal. We have a unique opportunity to lower rates and introduce competition in a reasonable time frame, if we establish a process to work together.

While the Concord Monitor, The Union Leader and The Keene Sentinel all suggested that the state take PSNH up on the proposal, The Keene Sentinel reported on June 15, "Within minutes, the offer was rejected by the governor [Steven Merrill] and most of the candidates to succeed him, Democratic and Republican."

To more clearly understand its role under the new statute, the Public Utilities Commission requested clarification from the New Hampshire Supreme Court as to whether it had the power to set rates that would reduce PSNH's rates below those agreed upon in the legislation supporting the bankruptcy agreement. It was not until December 23, 1998, over 2 ½ years after PSNH's *Customers First* proposal, that the court ruled affirmatively on this question. In the interim there was much action both within the courts and in private negotiations.

The mechanism used to circumvent the 1990 rate agreement was in that portion of the statute dealing with the rights of utilities to have their rates include a return on "stranded costs." The statute defined the term as follows:

> "Stranded costs" means costs... that electric utilities would reasonably expect to recover if the existing regulatory structure with retail rates for bundled provision of electric service continued...

However, when the Commission acted on the stranded cost portion of the restructuring statute, it did not use an accounting cost basis for determining rates. In place, the PUC introduced a "regional average rate benchmark." In the process, PSNH saw its proposed rates slashed. In response, it sued in the Federal Court. After a prolonged litigation process, an out-of-court agreement was reached on June 14, 1999. On that date a Memorandum of Understanding was reached between PSNH and the State of New Hampshire. The agreement called for PSNH to lower rates and introduce choice of energy suppliers. In addition, PSNH agreed to suspend all pending litigation and to withdraw its lawsuit against the NHPUC on the effective date of the final agreement.

On August 2, fewer then two months after the Memorandum of Understanding was signed, a final agreement was filed with state regulators. The agreement had the support of Governor Jeanne Shaheen, PSNH and NU, the Office of the Attorney General, the Governor's Office of Energy and Community Service and the staff of the NH-PUC. The agreement then required approval by the NHPUC. It also required the New Hampshire Legislature to approve the use of rate reduction bonds. It would take an additional twenty-one months for the process to be completed.

Gary Long

In the interim, on July 1, 2000, William Frain, Jr., retired. Gary Long, another long-term PSNH employee, was named president. Long holds a bachelor's degree in electrical engineering from New Mexico State University and a master's degree from Northeastern University. Long joined PSNH in 1976 following service as an officer in the United States Air Force. Prior to becoming president, Long held numerous positions with PSNH in marketing, customer service, regulatory affairs, economic development and rates.

In September 2000, the NHPUC approved the agreement in which PSNH agreed to write off $450 million of its $2.3 billion in old investments, associated with stranded costs. In addition, PSNH would reduce rates 5 percent in October with an additional 11 percent reduction on "Competition Day," scheduled for April, 1, 2001. In exchange, PSNH was allowed to refinance up to $800 million of its debt at lower interest rates, with the agreement that both interest and principal would be incorporated in the new lower customer rates.

Two of the most vocal groups against Public Service throughout the entire Seabrook issue were the Campaign for Ratepayers Rights and the Granite State Taxpayers Association. Both groups opposed granting PSNH any stranded costs. In effect, they wanted to force the company to write off all $2.3 billion. The two groups appealed the decision to the New Hampshire Supreme Court. On January 16, 2001, the New Hampshire Supreme Court rejected the appeal to overturn the NHPUC order to deregulate PSNH. Said PSNH President Gary Long:

This is a very significant day for our customers and the company. Our customers have waited a long time for this rate reduction and we are very pleased that the court rejected the attempt to block it. We will now move ahead to implement the deregulation settlement, including customer choice, as soon as possible... We will continue to work with the State Legislature and regulators to ensure that the process moves forward in a manner which provides our customers with long-term benefits. Our goal is to make the transition as smooth as possible for our customers.

However, the groups opposing the agreement did not stop. They carried their cause all the way to the United States Supreme Court. At this stage most newspapers throughout the state supported the agreement, and were calling for the groups to drop their lawsuits. The issue was finally resolved on Monday, May 14, 2001, when the court refused to take up the petition of the two groups.

This latter court petition further complicated the rate agreement. In responding to the U.S. Supreme Court decision, PSNH spokesperson Martin Murray made the following comment, "We've known from the beginning the appeal had absolutely no merit, but it cost us and our customers time and money." The delay moved "Competition Day" from April 1 to May 1, 2001. On that day an 11 percent rate reduction went into effect. This was in addition to the 5 percent drop back on October 1, 2000. Rates dropped a total of 16 percent, and in theory customer choice of energy suppliers began. For the first time in many years retail customers saw their bills drop below the regional average.

Perhaps the most dramatic and long-term implication of the 1996 restructuring act was requiring PSNH to separate its transmission and distribution operation from its generating function. In effect PSNH was to sell its generating facilities to non-Northeast Utilities power suppliers. This portion of the act appears to have been motivated by the assumption that competition on a regional or a national scale for power generation would result in lower cost for that portion of one's total electric bill.

By the time that the final PSNH rate reduction was resolved, the State of California was experiencing substantial difficulty under its deregulation. Retail suppliers, who were required to deliver electricity to retail customers at a fixed rate, saw the cost of purchasing electricity increase far in excess of the fixed retail price. This was followed by rolling blackouts, and major electric utilities filing for bankruptcy.

In the spring of 2001, the New Hampshire Legislature was beginning to have second thoughts on requiring PSNH to sell its non-Seabrook generating plants. At that time the cost of generating one's own power appeared to be the better alternative. On April 19, both the House and Senate passed House Bill 489, postponing the sale of PSNH's fossil-fuel and hydroelectric plants for thirty-three months. As a result of this law, "Competition Day," while significant with respect to the rate decrease, did not initiate the beginning of an active market in generating electric energy. On May 1, 2001, PSNH President Gary Long commented:

> Despite the fact that customers now have the ability to choose their energy supplier, the reality is that it will likely take some time for a robust retail electric marketplace to develop. The good news is that the mechanisms are now in place to support this market as it evolves in the future and to protect our customers with low rates and a reliable supply of power in the meantime.

Following PSNH's seventy-fifth anniversary in August of 2001, four significant events occurred. First, in March 2002 PSNH moved into Energy Park, its new corporate headquarters. The location is the renovated Manchester Steam Plant originally constructed by the Amoskeag Manufacturing Company in 1909, and acquired by PSNH in the Amoskeag bankruptcy in 1936. The plant provided electric power for PSNH until 1981 when it was taken out of service. In 2000, the company announced its plans to renovate and preserve the integrity of the dormant building, while creating a state-of-the-art office complex.

Later in the same year, the Seabrook Nuclear Power Plant was sold to Florida Power and Light. This apparent separation of ownership of production facilities and location of retail customers was in response the national movement towards deregulation. In a Boston Globe column, Charles Stern noted:

> The Seabrook nuclear power plant in New Hampshire was sold last week. The story attracted almost no attention, which is a story in itself. For almost 20 years, from early 1970s to the early 1990s, Seabrook was front page news. For a variety of reasons, it became one of the nation's key

battlegrounds in the fight over nuclear power. People who loved nuclear power strove mightily rebuild it; people who loathed nukes worked just as hard to kill the project....

At Seabrook, both sides were sure their view of the future was the right one....

Nuclear power is a mixed bag. It hasn't solved all our problems, or destroyed the world. The subject still generates plenty of passion, however.

The third significant event occurred when PSNH, announced plans to purchase Connecticut Valley Electric Co. for $30 million from its parent corporation, Central Vermont Public Service Co. CVEV services two separate areas in the western part of New Hampshire, all located on the Connecticut River. The southern location in Sullivan County services Claremont. The more northerly location services the Grafton County communities of Lyme, Orford, Piermont, Haverhill and Bath. The NHPUC approved the plan on May 23, 2003. As of the date of this book, final details of the acquisition have not been completed. PSNH announced plans to lower rates in these communities by about 15 percent. Dennis C. Delay, former long-term economist with PSNH, noted, "This represents a final step in PSNH's evolution from its bankruptcy. Once again the company is expanding the area in which it is providing electricity to New Hampshire."

The final significant event following PSNH's celebration of its seventy-fifth anniversary occurred on April 23, 2003, when Governor Craig Benson signed Senate Bill 170 extending until April 30, 2006, the time period that PSNH would be allowed to keep its power plants. Once again New Hampshire Legislature was reassessing the proposed separation of the generation of electricity from the transmission and supplying of the utility to customers in light of the continuing problems experienced in California.

It may take well into the second century of the history of Manchester Traction, Light and Power Co. and Public Service Co. of New Hampshire to evaluate that portion of the deregulation act that called for the breaking up of an integrated electric company.

PSNH Energy Park, 2002

Epilogue

In 1830, German philosopher G.W.F. Hegel wrote, "What experience and history teach is this–that nations and governments have never learned anything from history, or acted upon any lesson that might have drawn from it." Seventy-five years later, Spanish-born philosopher George Santayana wrote, "Those who cannot remember the past are condemned to repeat it." Contemporary American philosopher Lawrence Peter 'Yogi' Berra said it more succinctly, "Déjà vu all over again." Because so little attention is paid to business history by investors and the entrepreneurs attracted to opportunities found in emerging industries, by government officials charged with regulating and overseeing competition, and by the general public as to what factors motivate companies interested in long run results, these quotes are particularly poignant.

Nowhere is history disregarded more than in the field of investing. Each generation views the new industries of its era as significantly different from all previous innovations, promising unlimited growth, an infinite life and freedom from the perils of economic slowdowns. While some investors and the individuals with whom they have placed their savings will view in proper perspective the opportunities surrounding a new industry, others will overreact as a result of irrational projections of future growth potential.

In this respect, the trolley innovation was no exception. For the most part, the financing by Tucker, Anthony and Co. and the executive leadership under J. Brodie Smith kept Manchester Traction, Light and

Power Co.'s expectations in check. The Manchester Street Railway and the Manchester and Nashua Street Railway ran profitably for many years. In retrospect, however, the Manchester and Derry Street Railroad never should have been built. On the other hand the financing provided by the New York Security & Trust Co. and the flamboyant overexpansion by Wallace D. Lovell of the Exeter, Hampton and Amesbury System proved a perfect formula for guaranteeing unprofitable operations. In effect, this investment appears to have been based on the assumption that trolleys would be profitable regardless of where they were built. Such a mind set did not end with the demise of the trolley industry. History has repeated itself with each generation, resulting in irrational overinvesting and subsequent losses in personal wealth. The most recent incident involved the unbounded expectations surrounding the Internet and "dot coms".

While the investing community has difficulty in learning from its past mistakes, government bodies have difficulty in learning from past successes. For a century, the electric utility industry improved service at lower real costs when compared with overall inflation by integrating horizontally and vertically. In addition, the industry provided further economies and safety valves by forming alliances like the New England Power Pool. In exchange for the opportunity to seek the gains of lower average costs associated with large-scale operations, the industry embraced regulation. National leaders like Samuel Insull and regional leaders like Avery Schiller preached the creed of large-scale integration through private ownership under government regulations.

Despite the apparent long-run success of a fully integrated industry, the current theory in vogue is to force power distributors to sell off their generating facilities, in the hope that competition between alternative power producers will lower costs. In effect the plan calls for deregulating the producing end and continuing to regulate the distribution end of the business. While it is premature to pass judgment on the program in New Hampshire, results when this book went to press for California indicate that serious problems could emerge.

If investors and entrepreneurs can be criticized for "irrational exuberance" and government regulators can be criticized for "over tinkering," the general public should be criticized for failing to understand "profit maximization" as practiced by businessmen and businesswomen interested in long-run results. To a great extent, the blame must be placed on the economists who teach monopoly theory and the newspapers that campaign against big business.

In Chapter 6, J.P. Morgan was quoted as saying, "An individual does something for two reasons, a good reason and the real reason." In effect, Morgan would have attributed all of Dewing's four reasons, discussed in Chapters 7 and 14, as the real reason. Since three of Dewing's real reasons are ego-based, they must be held in check. Individuals who have directed firms that have survived the test of time in a competitive market can attribute their companies' successes in attaining the "real reasons," profitability and the admiration of the public, to their concentration on the "good reasons," suppling a quality product or service at a fair price, providing continual employment to its workers at a just wage, and demonstrating a genuine interest in the community in which it operates.

That is not to say that all firms will act honorably. Nor does it imply that within a socially conscious firm certain individuals will not make inappropriate decisions. Rather, it suggests that firms that have succeeded in maximizing their long-run profitability have done so by de-emphasizing their short-run profit goals and concentrating on the "good reasons." For a century, Manchester Traction, Light and Power Co. and Public Service Co. of New Hampshire concentrated on the "good reasons."

On the other hand, concentration on the "good reasons" does not guarantee economic success. Occasionally, factors beyond the scope of reasonable expectations will cause the best intended plans to go wrong. Such was the case with respect to Seabrook.

Chronological Summary

1852   Manchester Gas Co. began providing the city with gas lights.

1864   New Hampshire Legislature chartered Manchester Horse Railroad.

1871   Manchester Horse Railroad organized but did not begin construction of lines until 1877.

1877   Manchester Horse Railroad began operations.

1881   Manchester Electric Light Co. organized. The company failed to raise sufficient funds to build a power plant to provide electricity for city electric arc lights.

1882   New England Weston Electric Light Co. of Boston provided power for city's arc lights from power purchased from Amoskeag Manufacturing Co.

1883   New England Weston Electric Light Co. of Boston completed construction of its own steam power plant in Manchester in February.

1885   New England Weston Electric Light Co. purchased shares of Manchester Electric Light Co. and transferred Manchester steam-power plant to that firm.

1886   Ben Franklin Electric Co. organized to provide steam-generated electricity to Manchester in competition with Manchester
Electric Light Co. J. Brodie Smith was its manager.

1886   Nashua Electric Light Co. organized.

1889   General Charles Williams gained control of Manchester Horse
Railway. The name was changed to Manchester Street Railroad.

1890   The Electric Co., a third provider of electricity in Manchester
was organized providing power from its Kelley's Falls hydroelectric plant. Over the next three years, three additional
electric companies were formed. The Merrimack Electric
Light, Heat and Power Co. formed in 1891, began generating hydroelectric power from Hooksett beginning in 1895.
The Garvin's Falls Power Co. began providing hydroelectric
power in 1892. The Union Electric Company was organized
in 1893 at which time it absorbed The Electric Co.

1892   Manchester Electric Light Co. acquired the Ben Franklin Electric Co. The following year J. Brodie Smith was appointed
the superintendent of the consolidated firm.

1895   Manchester Horse Railway electrified.

1895   New seasonal line opened to Massabesic Lake. Pleasure ori-
entation.

1896   Manchester Electric Co. organized. Over the next four years
it would absorb Garvin's Falls Power Co., Union Electric
Co. and the Merrimack Electric Light, Heat and Power Co.
thereby reducing the number of independent electric power
companies to two: the Manchester Electric Light Co. and the
Manchester Electric Co.

1898   Tucker, Anthony & Co., an investment firm in Boston acquired
control of the Manchester Street Railway. About the same time
it acquired control of Manchester's two power companies.

1899   J. Brodie Smith appointed superintendent of the Manchester Street Railway while continuing to serve as superintendent of the Manchester Electric Light Co.

1901   Manchester Traction, Light and Power Co. (MTL&P) incorporated August 16. Under the direction of Tucker, Anthony & Co., the firm absorbed the Manchester Electric Light Co., and the Manchester Electric Co. The firm also acquired control of the Manchester Street Railway through stock ownership.

Amoskeag Manufacturing Co. contracted with MTL&P to provide its new plant with electric power. The plant, located on the west side of the river, could not be supplied with water power from the canals located on the east side.

1902   Pine Island Park opened at the end of the Goffs Falls line of the Manchester Street Railway. The amusement park, built by Manchester Traction, Light and Power Co., in addition to providing revenue from its various concessions, increased trolley traffic on weekends.

1903   The tracks of the Manchester Street Railway were connected with the Concord & Manchester Electric Branch of the Boston & Maine Railroad. While the two firms were run separately, this allowed Concord trolleys to run to downtown Manchester.

1906   MTL&P ran railway lines from Manchester to Nashua, Londonderry and Derry by way of two new corporations; Manchester and Nashua Street Railway began operations in early 1907, and the Manchester and Derry Street Railway started running later the same year.

1907   Uncanoonuc Mountain Cable Co. began operation.

1915   Trolleys experienced new competition from jitneys.

1922   Amoskeag Manufacturing Co. built a 16,000-kilowatt steam plant to provide energy for its textile mills.

1926 Public Service of New Hampshire (PSNH) incorporated August 16. The firm brought together MTL&P, Keene Gas & Electric Co., Ashuelot Gas & Electric Co., Laconia Gas & Electric Co. and Souhegan Valley Electric Co.

1927 PSNH acquired Southern New Hampshire Hydro-Electric Corp. and Conway Electric Light & Power.

1928 PSNH acquired Franklin Light and Power Co., Tilton Electric and Power Co. and Utility Power Co.

1929 PSNH purchased water power and steam plant of Great Falls Manufacturing Co. Stock Market Crash marked the beginning of the Great Depression.

1930 PSNH purchased Eastman Falls Hydroelectric plant on the Pemigewasset River at Franklin, NH from the Boston and Maine Railroad for $600,000.

PSNH acquired Bethlehem Electric Co., Lisbon Light and Power Co., Compton Electric Light Co. and Freedom Electric Co.

1931 PSNH purchased Jacona, a 20,000-kilowatts floating power ship, from Marine Power Co. PSNH discontinued operations of the Manchester and Nashua Street Railway in September.

Insull lost control of Middle West Utilities Co., which was in receivership. Middle West loses control of New England Public Service Co., and all of its subsidiaries, including PSNH. Public Service continues as a subsidiary of NEPSCo until 1946.

1932 Insull tried for mail fraud and later tried for embezzlement. In both trials, he was found not guilty.

1933 Legislation passed limiting power of public utility holding companies.

PSNH acquired Groveton Electric Light Co. and Lyman Falls Power Co. from its parent company, New England Public Service Co.

1935   Amoskeag Manufacturing Co. closed its mills and files for voluntary reorganization.

1936   Amoskeag Manufacturing Co. filed for bankruptcy. PSNH purchases Amoskeag's 16,000-kilowatt steam power plant and all of the textile water rights for $2.25 million.

PSNH acquired New Hampshire Power Co. from Middle West Corp. and Electric Security Corp.

1939   PSNH acquired Watson Williams Manufacturing Co. and Frank M. Baldwin Co.

1940   PSNH discontinued Manchester trolley system and replaced service with busses.

PSNH acquired electric distribution property and rights for Brookline and Hollis from New Hampshire Gas & Electric.

NEPSCo. ordered by SEC to either liquefy its assets or simplify its capital structure.

1941   Avery R. Schiller replaced J. Brodie Smith as general manager of PSNH.

1942   Schiller named PSNH's president and general manager. This was the first time in the 41-year history of MTL&P and PSNH the president was a local internal officer of the firm.

1943   PSNH purchased Twin State Gas and Electric Co, servicing communities along the Maine-New Hampshire border.

1945   U.S. military requisitioned PSNH's Jacona.

PSNH purchased Wonalancet Electric Co. and the Wakefield

Power Co.

1946 For the first time PSNH's common stock was sold to the general public.

PSNH purchased Resistance, a 30,000-kilowatt floating power plant in a government liquidation of excess military facilities following the end of the war.

PSNH purchased hydroelectric plant from George H. Jones.

PSNH sold all gas facilities to Gas Services, Inc.

1948 PSNH completed 15,000-kilowatt hydroelectric plant named after J. Brodie Smith.

PSNH purchased electric distribution system of Town of Hancock.

1949 New Hampshire Public Utilities Commission authorized PSNH to add to their electric rates a "fuel and purchasing power adjustment."

PSNH completed 40,000-kilowt steam plant in Portsmouth named after Avery R. Schiller.

1950 PSNH sold retail distribution facilities in Enfield-Canaan to Granite State Electric Co.

1951 Schiller wrote a letter to shareholders, customers and employees expressing concern over attempts to socialize public utilities.

PSNH's Annual Report for 1950, published in 1951, included an explanation of the limited role of water power in the future.

1952 Capacity of Schiller plant doubled to 80,000 kilowatts.

1954 PSNH purchased New Hampshire Electric Co.

Yankee Atomic Energy Co. formed by PSNH and 11 other New England utilities to construct a nuclear power plant in Rowe, Massachusetts.

1956 PSNH purchased municipal electric distribution facilities in Rindge.

Construction began on a new 100,000-kilowatt Merrimack Plant in Bow, N.H.

1957 Schiller plant capacity increased to 172,000 kilowatts.

PSNH sold Manchester bus system to Manchester Transit, Inc.

1960 Coal-fired 100,000-kilowatt Merrimack Plant, in Bow, N.H., went into operation in October.

1961 Resistance sold to Korean Electric Co.

1966 Ground broken for Merrimack II with a projected capacity of 350,000 kilowatts.

1967 Eleven major electric utility firms throughout New England agreed to form New England Power Pool [NEPOOL] to formalize cooperative sharing of power.

1968 Merrimack II went on line May 1.

PSNH announced plans for construction of 860,000-kilowatt nuclear plant in Seabrook, N.H. on May 20.

1969 Seabrook Plant put on hold.

1970 Ground breaking for 400,000-kilowatt oil-fired plant in Newington, N.H.

PSNH stock registered on the New York Stock Exchange. Trading on the "Big Board" began on September 16.

1971 PSNH filed for first rate increase since 1959. About half of the 13 percent requested increase was granted by the PUC which rescinded the fuel adjustment clause. . The company appealed to the N.H. Supreme Court. On December 31, 1974 the PUC approved the 1971 request.

1973 PSNH applied to Atomic Energy Commission for permission to build twin unit plant at Seabrook - March 30.

1974 Newington Plant put on line June 30.

1975 Environmental Protection Agency approved Seabrook cooling system which would utilize ocean water–June 24.

1976 Seabrook residents voted against construction of nuclear plant 768 to 632–March 2.

Nuclear Regulatory Commission granted construction permit–July 7. The commission subsequently reversed decision, calling for a moratorium until national standards on nuclear waste were established.

Clamshell Alliance formed with intention of stopping Seabrook construction–July 13.

Eighteen protesters from Clamshell Alliance arrested while attempting to occupy Seabrook–Aug. 1.

Seabrook groundbreaking ceremonies, 3 protesters arrested–Aug. 5.

179 protesters arrested in occupation of Seabrook site–Aug. 22.

Nuclear Regulatory Commission's appeal board suspended Seabrook permit–Sept. 27.

Nuclear Regulatory Commission reinstated Seabrook construction permit–Oct. 5.

Regional EPA Director rejected Seabrook's proposed cooling system–Nov. 8.

1977 NRC Appeals Board halted Seabrook construction because of question on cooling system–Jan. 21.

Largest nuclear protest in history to that date. 1,414 Seabrook protesters arrested–May 1.

National EPA director overruled regional decision and approved cooling system–June 17.

NRC Appeals Board reinstated Seabrook construction permit–July 26.

1978 Federal Appeals Court in Boston objected to EPA procedure and sent cooling issue back to EPA–Feb. 15.

Clamshell Alliance protest drew 10,000 demonstrators–June 24.

NRC suspended construction permit because of cooling system issue–June 30.

EPA reaffirmed approval of cooling system–Aug. 4.

NRC reinstated construction permit–Aug. 11.

Five separate protesting incidences at Seabrook. A total of 93 protesters arrested–Aug. 14 through Oct. 7.

1979 183 Seabrook protesters arrested for blocking delivery of equipment–Mar. 9.

"Turning Tide" demonstration by Clamshell Alliance. About 2,300 attended peaceful rally–July 21-22.

Twenty-two arrested when 2,000 demonstrators attempted to take over Seabrook. Police resorted to Mace, tear gas and guard dogs for the first time–Oct. 6-10.

Citing financial difficulties, PSNH attempted to sell 10 percent of its holdings in Seabrook–Oct. 15.

PSNH announced that it would delay second Seabrook reactor 4 years–Nov. 14.

NHPUC granted PSNH $11.9 emergency rate increase–Dec. 21.

1980 Half of Seabrook construction workers laid off in attempt to preserve capital–March 20.

R.J. Harrison appointed president of PSNH. Tallman's position changed from President and CEO to Chairman and CEO.

Violent protests at Seabrook - May 24 & 25.

1986 Unit I of Seabrook completed in July. Because of legal delays, the plant did not go on line until August, 1990.

1988 N.H. Supreme Court upheld the Anti-CWIP law on January, 26.

PSNH filed for bankruptcy protection on January, 28.

Northeast Utilities declared interest in acquiring PSNH–March 24.

John C. Duffett appointed PSNH's president replacing Harrison who resigned for health reasons–Sept 15.

1989 NU filed a reorganization plan for PSNH with the federal bankruptcy court–Mar. 22.

Gov. Judd Gregg endorsed NU's reorganization plan–July 27.

U.S. Bankruptcy Judge James Yacos declared PSNH can seek reorganization under Federal Energy Regulatory Commission freeing it from NH PUC oversight–Sept. 23

NU plan received support of major creditors and stock-holders–Nov. 18.

N.H. Legislature endorsed NU plan - Dec. 14.

1990   First of seven scheduled 5.5 percent increases in PSNH's rates took effect.

U.S. Bankruptcy Court confirmed the NU plan, including a Rate Agreement with the State of New Hampshire, (SofNH)– April 20.

Following a six-month review, the NHPUC approved the Rate Agreement.

Seabrook Station began 100 percent commercial operation–Aug. 19.

1991   New Hampshire Supreme Court upheld the Rate Agreement and NU's plan to acquire PSNH; PSNH emerged from bankruptcy–May 16.

1992   Northeast Utilities completed its acquisition of PSNH. R. Frank Locke of NU is appointed PSNH president.

1994   William T. Frain, Jr., a Manchester native and 30-year PSNH veteran, appointed PSNH president by NU, replacing Frank Locke upon his retirement–Feb. 1.

Freedom Electric Power Co. filed petition with NHPUC requesting approval to serve and compete for PSNH's retail customers–Aug.

1995   NHPUC initiated a series of "roundtable meetings" to consider electric utility competition.

PSNH and SofNH engaged in discussions aimed at renegotiating the Rate Agreement. Discussions ended without a resolution of major issues–March-June.

NHPUC ruled that franchises in New Hampshire are not exclusive as a matter of law. Ruling opened way for Freedom to compete with PSNH for retail customers. PSNH appealed ruling to NH Supreme Court–June.

1996   NH Supreme Court upheld NHPUC's ruling on non-exclusive franchising–May.

NH legislature passed restructuring law (HB 1392) calling for unbundling of generating facilities from transmission and distribution facilities. Generating facilities to be based on competitive market model. Transmission and distribution facilities to remain regulated. Pilot program for competition in supplying energy began–May 21.

1996   Final 5.5 percent PSNH rate increase took effect, as per Rate Agreement–June 1.

1997   NHPUC issued restructuring plan requiring utilities to sell generating plants, restricting utilities from selling power to their current customers, and limiting utilities' ability to recover past investments in future rates–Feb. 28.

PSNH petitioned federal court for restraining order to prevent implementation of NHPUC's restructuring plan–Mar. 3.

PSNH and SofNH engaged in court-approved mediation process on rate issue and deregulation process. Mediation ended without resolution–May-Sept.

1998   NHPUC issued revised order on restructuring, with a new PSNH stranded cost recovery rate to be set in future–Mar 20.

NHPUC extended indefinitely the state's electric utility retail pilot program–May 26.

U.S. District Court (USDC) issued preliminary injunction, prohibiting NHPUC from proceeding with restructuring or implementing involuntary restructuring plans–June 12.

PSNH, the N.H. Governor's Office of Energy and Community Service, and staff members from NHPUC began discussion aimed at setting outstanding issues and achieving a restructuring agreement–Aug.

1999   A Memorandum of Understanding reached between PSNH and SofNH in which PSNH would lower rates 18 percent, introduce choice of energy suppliers and suspend pending litigation–June 14.

N.H. Legislature approved a bill allowing NHPUC to review and approve settlement agreement subject to legislative final approval–July 1.

Final agreement aimed at significantly reducing electric rates for PSNH customers filed with NHPUC. The agreement supported by N.H. Governor Shaheen, PSNH and NU, the Office of N.H. Attorney General, the Governor's Office of Energy and Community Service, and the staff of NHPUC–Aug. 2.

NHPUC scheduled a two-step process to consider the PSNH restructuring agreement - Aug. 10. In Phase One, proponents of plan presented testimony–Oct.-Nov. In Phase Two, opponents of the plan presented testimony–Nov., 1999-Feb., 2000.

2000   PSNH filed, with the NHPUC, its final brief in support of the proposed rate reduction and restructuring agreement–Mar. 3.

NHPUC approved a modified PSNH restructuring agreement, substantially changing some aspects of the Aug. 2, 1999 agreement–April 19. PSNH requested a motion for rehearing–May 1.

N.H. House of Representatives voted in favor of a plan to refinance PSNH debt, driving forward the deal to cut electric rates and introduce competition in energy production–May 17.

N.H. House and Senate approved legislation (SB 472) aimed at lowering PSNH rates and allowing customers to choose an energy supplier - May 31. N.H. Gov. Jeanne Shaheen signed bill into law–June 12. Action by NHPUC still necessary prior to implementation.

Gary Long appointed PSNH president, replacing William Frain, Jr., upon his retirement–July 1.

PSNH reduced rates 5 percent in line with restructuring agreement–Oct. 1.

Campaign for Ratepayers Rights (CRR) and Granite State Taxpayers Assoc. (GSTA) filed appeals with N.H. Supreme Court, opposing NHPUC restructuring order–Oct. 10.

PSNH filed company's "Divestiture Plan" with the NHPUC. The plan called for the sale of all fossil-fueled and hydro-electric generating facilities owned by PSNH. In addition, NU's subsidiary, North Atlantic Energy Corp., required to sell its ownership in Seabrook–Dec. 15.

2001 N.H. Supreme Court, rejected Oct. 10, 2000 appeals, upholding PSNH deregulation plan - Jan. 16. The parties filed with the U.S. Supreme Court which refused to consider the appeal.

Deregulation plan put into effect, reducing PSNH's rates an additional 10 percent.

New Hampshire Legislature passed House Bill 489 postponing the sale of PSNH's fossil-fuel and hydroelectric plants for 33 months - April 19.

PSNH celebrates its 75th anniversary.

2002 PSNH moves its corporate headquarters into Energy Park, the renovated Manchester Steam plant.

Seabrook Nuclear Power Plant sold to Florida Power & Light.

PSNH announces plan to purchase Connecticut Valley Electric Co.

2003 Governor Craig Benson signs Senate Bill 170 extending until April 30, 2006, time period that PSNH would be allowed to keep its power plants.-April 2003.

NHPUC Approves Planned Acquisition of Connecticut Valley Electric Co.-May 23.

Bibliography

Cummings, O.R., "Berlin Street Railway," *Electric Traction Quarterly,* Vol. 3, No. 3, Spring, 1965.

Cummings, O.R., "The Dover, Somersworth & Rochester Street Railway," *Transportation*, Vol. 3, July-December 1949.

Cummings, O.R., "Exeter, Hampton & Amesbury Street Railway," *Transportation,* Vol. 5, 1951.

Cummings, O.R. & the Manchester Historic Association, *Images of America: Manchester Streetcars,* Arcadia Publishing, 2000.

Cummings, O.R., "Manchester Streetcars 1877-1940", unpublished.

Cummings, O.R., "Manchester Street Railways," Electric Railway Historical Society, No. 35, March 1960.

Cummings, O.R., "Portsmouth Electric Railway," *Election Traction Quarterly,* Vol. 5, Nos. 1 & 2, Fall & Winter 1966.

Cummings, O.R., "Queen City Horsecar Days," Monograph, 1976.

Cummings, O.R., "Trolleys to the Casino - Exeter, Hampton & Amesbury Street Railway," Monograph, New England Electric Railway Historical Society, Inc., 1969.

Danielian, N.R., "From Insull to Injury: A Study in Financial Jugglery," *The Atlantic Monthly,* April 1933.

Dewing, Arthur Stone, *The Financial Policy of Corporations,* The Roland Press Co., 1920.

Ely, Richard T., *Socialism, an Examination of Its Nature, Its Strength and Its Weakness, with Suggestions for Social Reform*, 6th ed., T.Y. Crowell & Co., 1894.

Flynn, John T., "What Happened to Insull," *The New Republic, May 4, 1932.*

Hunt, Roger W., "Predecessors of Public Service Company of New Hampshire," Unpublished PSNH, 1976.

Irwin, Jr., Clark T., *The Light from the River: Central Maine Power's First Century of Service,* Central Maine Power Co., 1999.

Kenison, Arthur M., *Dumaine's Amoskeag: Let the Record Speak,* Saint Anselm College Press, 1997.

Kenison, Arthur M., *Frederic C. Dumaine: Office Boy to Tycoon,* Saint Anselm College Press, 2000.

Lawrence, Loring M., "Manchester," *Motor Coach Age,* October 1973.

Lawrence, Loring M., "Manchester Update," *Motor Coach Age,* June 1977.

Manchester Union Leader, 1968 - 2001.

Mason, Francis M., *The Manchester Gas Company: A brief history of the first 125 years of gas in Manchester,* 1977.

McDonald, Forest, *Insull,* The University of Chicago Press, 1962.

Miller, John Anderson, *Fares, Please! From Horse-Cars to Stream-liners,* D. Appleton-Century Co., 1941.

Moody's Public Utilities Manual, 1914 - 2000.

New Hampshire Sunday News, 1968 - 2001.

Phillips, Jr., Charles F., *The Regulation of Public Utilities: Theory and Practice,* Public Utility Reports, Inc., 1988.

Public Service Co. of New Hampshire - archives.

Ramsay, M.L., *Pyramids of Power: The Story of Roosevelt, Insull and the Utility Wars,* The Bobbs-Merrill Co., 1937.

Romps, John, "Comments on Public Service Co. of New Hampshire's Bankruptcy," Unpublished.

Rowsome, Jr., Frank, *Trolley Car Treasury,* McGraw-Hill Book Co., Inc., 1956.

Rukeyser, Merryle Stanley, *The Common Sense of Money and Investing,* Simon and Schuster, 1924.

Sackette, Everett B., *Fifty Years of Service: a History of Public Service Co. of New Hampshire,* Public Service Co. of New Hampshire, 1976.

Schiller, Avery R., "Amber Forever," Newcomen Society, 1950.

Skelton, William B., "Walter S. Wyman (1874-1942) - One of Maine's Great Pioneers," Newcomen Society , 1949.

Straw, Colonel William Parker, "Amoskeag in New Hampshire: an Epic in American Industry," Newcomen Society, 1948.

Wells, Edward O., "Sunk Costs," *New England Monthly,* July 1990

Index

A

Amory, William 7
Amesbury & Hampton Railroad 33
Amoskeag Industries 66-69
Amoskeag Manufacturing Co. 6, 12, 28, 63-69, 134
amusement parks 3, 13-14, 17-19, 34, 41
Anthony, S. Reed 17
Anti-CWIP 105, 110, 117, 121-122, 123-124
anti-nuclear protests 104-107
Ashuelot Gas and Electric Co. 22, 38, 50
Associated Gas and Electric Co. 37
atomic energy, see nuclear energy
Atomic Safety and Licensing Board 103

B

Bankruptcy 109-113
Ben Franklin Electric Light Co. 10, 12-13
Benson, Craig 135
Berlin Electric Co. 40
Berlin Paper Co. 40
Berlin Street Railway 40-41
Berra, Lawrence Peter "Yogi" 137
Bethlehem Electric Co. 52
Bohan, Todd M. 77-78, 124, 128
Boston and Maine Railroad 52
Boston Edison 125
Boston Industrial Co. 38
Brown Paper Co. 40-41
Burgett, H.W. 36-37
Burke, Thomas 84
Bus service 3 , 24, 37, 40, 41, 71-72, 84

C

Cable car system 20-21
Campaign for Ratepayers Rights 132-133
Carney, Joseph 65
Cascade Electric Light & Power Co. 40-41
Cascade Park 41
Central Maine Power Co. 52-53, 61, 75, 111
Central Vermont Public Service Corp. 61, 75, 111, 135
Cheshire Transportation Co. 40
Chicago Edison Co. 44
Citizens Electric Co. 38

Exeter Railway & Lighting Co. 35
Exeter Street Railway 32-33

F

Federal Energy Regulatory Commission 110
Frain, Jr., William 95, 107, 126-128
Franklin Light and Power Co. 51
Freedom Electric Co. 52
Freedom Electric Power Co. 128
Florida Power and Light 134

G

Gallen, Hugh 105, 106, 117, 118, 123
Garvin's Falls Power Co. 12, 14
Gas Services, Inc. 77
General Electric Co. 44
Gorham Electric Light Co. 40
Government ownership 77-81, 83-84, 97
Government regulation see regulation
Granite State Electric Co. 83
Granite State Taxpayers Association 132-133
Great Depression 1, 55, 57, 63-69
Great Falls Manufacturing Co. 52
Greenville Electric Lighting Co. 97
Gregg, Judd 110-112
Gross, Edward 41
Groveton Electric Light Co. 53

H

Hallidie, Andrew S. 20
Hampton & Amesbury Street Railway 32-34
Hampton Beach Casino and Ocean House 34
Harrison, R.J. 106, 108, 111
Hegel, G.W.F. 137
Horse-drawn railways 3, 5-9, 36, 38
Hydro-electricity 11-12, 51-52, 68-69, 76, 79-80, 82, 83, 85-86, 109
Hydro-Quebec 109

I

Insull Utilities Investments 58-61
Insull, Martin 45-46, 51, 72
Insull, Samuel 43-47, 57-61, 127, 138

J

Jacona 52-53, 76
Jitney services 23-24
Jones, George H. 76
Junk bonds 117-119

K

L

M

Thomas A. Edison Construction Department 43
Thomson-Houston Co. 12, 36, 43-44
Thomson, Meldrim 105, 117
Tilton Electric and Power Co. 51
Trolley car systems 9, 13-15, 17-28, 31-41, 71-72
Tucker, Anthony & Co. 17, 50, 72, 137
Tucker, W.S. 17
Twin State Gas and Electric Co. 61, 75, 77
Tyrell, J.P. 125

U

Union Electric Co 11-12, 14.
Union Electric Railway 37
Union Street Railway (Dover) 37
Union Street Railway (Holding company) 84
United Illuminating Co. 92
Utility Power Co. 51

V

Vermont Yankee Nuclear Power Corp. 90

W

Wakefield Power Co. 77
Wells, Edward O. 116-122
Weston, James A.6.
Williams, Charles 9-10, 17
Wolfeboro municipal service 97
Wonalancet Electric Co. 77
Wright, Harry 47
Wyman, Walter S. 46, 51, 61, 73, 126

Y

Yacos, James 110-112, 122
Yankee Atomic Energy Co. 86-87, 89-90